UNDERSTANDING
DRUGS

Amphetamines and Methamphetamine

TITLES IN THE *UNDERSTANDING DRUGS* SERIES

UNDERSTANDING DRUGS

Amphetamines and Methamphetamine

CHRISTINE ADAMEC

CONSULTING EDITOR

DAVID J. TRIGGLE Ph.D.

University Professor
School of Pharmacy and Pharmaceutical Sciences
State University of New York at Buffalo

CHELSEA HOUSE
An Infobase Learning Company

Amphetamines and Methamphetamine

Chelsea House
An Infobase Learning Company
132 West 31st Street
New York NY 10001

Library of Congress Cataloging-in-Publication Data

Adamec, Christine A., 1949–
   Amphetamines and methamphetamine / Christine Adamec ; consulting editor, David J. Triggle.
      p. cm. — (Understanding drugs)
   Includes bibliographical references and index.
   ISBN-13: 978-1-60413-530-5 (hardcover : alk. paper)
   ISBN-10: 1-60413-530-1 (hardcover : alk. paper)   1. Amphetamines—Juvenile literature.   2. Methamphetamine—Juvenile literature.   3. Amphetamine abuse—Juvenile literature.   4. Methamphetamine abuse—Juvenile literature.   I. Triggle, D. J.   II. Title.   III. Series.
   RA1242.A5A33 2011
   362.29'9—dc22   2011011155

Text design by Kerry Casey
Cover design by Alicia Post
Composition by Newgen North America
Cover printed by Yurchak Printing, Landisville, Pa.
Book printed and bound by Yurchak Printing, Landisville, Pa.
Date printed: July 2011
Printed in the United States of America

10 9 8 7 6 5 4 3 2 1

Contents

foreword

THE USE AND ABUSE OF DRUGS

For thousands of years, humans have used a variety of sources with which to cure their ills, cast out devils, promote their well-being, relieve their misery, and control their fertility. Until the beginning of the twentieth century, the agents used were all of natural origin, including many derived from plants as well as elements such as antimony, sulfur, mercury, and arsenic. The sixteenth-century alchemist and physician Paracelsus used mercury and arsenic in his treatment of syphilis, worms, and other diseases that were common at that time; his cure rates, however, remain unknown. Many drugs used today have their origins in natural products. Antimony derivatives, for example, are used in the treatment of the nasty tropical disease leishmaniasis. These plant-derived products represent molecules that have been "forged in the crucible of evolution" and continue to supply the scientist with molecular scaffolds for new drug development.

Our story of modern drug discovery may be considered to start with the German physician and scientist Paul Ehrlich, often called the father of chemotherapy. Born in 1854, Ehrlich became interested in the ways in which synthetic dyes, then becoming a major product of the German fine chemical industry, could selectively stain certain tissues and components of cells. He reasoned that such dyes might form the basis for drugs that could interact selectively with diseased or foreign cells and organisms. One of Ehrlich's early successes was development of the arsenical "606"—patented under the name *Salvarsan*—as a treatment for syphilis. Ehrlich's goal was to create a "magic bullet," a drug that would target only the diseased cell or the invading disease-causing organism and have no effect on healthy cells and tissues. In this he was not successful, but his great research did lay the groundwork for the successes of the twentieth century, including the discovery of the sulfonamides and the antibiotic penicillin. The latter agent saved countless lives during

World War II. Ehrlich, like many scientists, was an optimist. On the eve of World War I, he wrote, "Now that the liability to, and danger of, disease are to a large extent circumscribed—the efforts of chemotherapeutics are directed as far as possible to fill up the gaps left in this ring." As we shall see in the pages of this volume, it is neither the first nor the last time that science has proclaimed its victory over nature, only to have to see this optimism dashed in the light of some freshly emerging infection.

From these advances, however, has come the vast array of drugs that are available to the modern physician. We are increasingly close to Ehrlich's magic bullet: Drugs can now target very specific molecular defects in a number of cancers, and doctors today have the ability to investigate the human genome to more effectively match the drug and the patient. In the next one to two decades, it is almost certain that the cost of "reading" an individual genome will be sufficiently cheap that, at least in the developed world, such personalized medicines will become the norm. The development of such drugs, however, is extremely costly and raises significant social issues, including equity in the delivery of medical treatment.

The twenty-first century will continue to produce major advances in medicines and medicine delivery. Nature is, however, a resilient foe. Diseases and organisms develop resistance to existing drugs, and new drugs must constantly be developed. (This is particularly true for anti-infective and anticancer agents.) Additionally, new and more lethal forms of existing infectious diseases can develop rapidly. With the ease of global travel, these can spread from Timbuktu to Toledo in less than 24 hours and become pandemics. Hence the current concerns with avian flu. Also, diseases that have previously been dormant or geographically circumscribed may suddenly break out worldwide. (Imagine, for example, a worldwide pandemic of Ebola disease, with public health agencies totally overwhelmed.) Finally, there are serious concerns regarding the possibility of man-made epidemics occurring through the deliberate or accidental spread of disease agents—including manufactured agents, such as smallpox with enhanced lethality. It is therefore imperative that the search for new medicines continue.

All of us at some time in our life will take a medicine, even if it is only aspirin for a headache or to reduce cosmetic defects. For some individuals, drug use will be constant throughout life. As we age, we will likely be exposed to a variety of medications—from childhood vaccines to drugs to relieve pain caused by a terminal disease. It is not easy to get accurate and understandable information about the drugs that we consume to treat diseases and disorders. There are, of course, highly specialized volumes aimed at medical or scientific professionals. These, however, demand a sophisticated knowledge base and experience to be comprehended. Advertising on television is widely available but provides only fleeting information, usually about only a single drug and designed to market rather than inform. The intent of this series of books, **Understanding Drugs,** is to provide the lay reader with intelligent, readable, and accurate descriptions of drugs, why and how they are used, their limitations, their side effects, and their future. The series will discuss both *"treatment drugs"*—typically, but not exclusively, prescription drugs, that have well-established criteria of both efficacy and safety—and *"drugs of abuse,"* agents that have pronounced pharmacological and physiological effects but that are, for a variety of reasons, not to be considered for therapeutic purposes. It is our hope that these books will provide readers with sufficient information to satisfy their immediate needs and to serve as an adequate base for further investigation and for asking intelligent questions of health care providers.

—David J. Triggle, Ph.D.
University Professor
School of Pharmacy and Pharmaceutical Sciences
State University of New York at Buffalo

1
Overview

*Jimmy, 16, had heard that the new kid Sam, 15, was taking Adderall for his attention-deficit/hyperactivity disorder—ADHD—and Jimmy decided to ask Sam for a few pills. Exams were coming up and Jimmy wanted an extra edge in school and thought maybe he could get such an advantage if he tried some of that Adderall he'd heard about. He was also curious about how the drug would affect him, truth be told. Sam knew few people at school and seemed lonely, so Jimmy thought if he acted like he'd be Sam's friend, then Sam would agree to share his pills. At first Sam was hesitant, but Jimmy said, "Come on, just five or six pills. I want to see if they can help me do better in school." Sam finally agreed, and next day at lunch in the cafeteria, Sam passed Jimmy the pills in an envelope. But a teacher saw the envelope transfer and also noted the guilt and panic on Sam's face. She snatched the envelope from a very startled Jimmy, and almost before the two boys knew what was happening, both were suspended from school for drugs. Jimmy said, "But it wasn't weed or crack or **crystal meth**! Just a few Adderall pills!" The principal said drugs weren't allowed in school and they also weren't allowed to be sold or given away to other kids. The suspension stood.*

Amphetamine and methamphetamine, a derivative of amphetamine—as well as methylphenidate (Ritalin, Concerta)—are central nervous system stimulants that primarily work on the brain, not only to cause the release of dopamine from nerve cells but also to block the removal of dopamine, thus increasing the total level of dopamine in the brain. Dopamine is a key brain chemical that affects a person's ability to feel and respond to pleasure, and it is also important for the mental and physical health of a person. To a lesser extent, amphetamines also increase the levels of norepinephrine and serotonin, two other key brain chemicals. For example, norepinephrine increases the heart rate and blood pressure and constricts the blood vessels. Serotonin is involved in mood control and more serotonin makes a person feel better. The difference between the normal levels of neurochemicals and the amplified levels induced by amphetamines is comparable to the difference between a whisper in the ear and a shout into a microphone.[1]

Central nervous system stimulants often cause the user to become more talkative, and more jittery because of the stimulation of muscles. Chronic abuse of these drugs can cause users to become delusional (believing things that are not true, such as that others are trying to harm the individual) or to hallucinate (seeing, hearing, or smelling things that are not there). Abuse of drugs such as methamphetamine can lead to increased aggression and a hypersexuality that increases the risk for dangerous behavior, such as having sex with multiple partners and not practicing safe sex.

The person who abuses amphetamines and especially methamphetamine is at risk for damage to every body system, including skin abscesses, severe dental problems, heart attack, pulmonary edema, liver damage, kidney failure, and a psychosis that is indistinguishable from paranoid schizophrenia.

After the person who abuses amphetamines or methamphetamine stops taking the drug, the body suddenly is depleted to a below-normal level of these chemicals and the individual feels depressed, apathetic, and extremely fatigued.[2] Depression and psychotic symptoms may persist for about a week with a sudden withdrawal from methamphetamine and the strong craving for the drug lasts a minimum of five weeks.[3]

Amphetamines and related stimulants are often used to treat children, adolescents, and adults with ADHD, and these medications are proven in numerous studies and books to help children, adolescents, and adults to better manage the impulsivity, inattentiveness, lack of concentration, and the hyperactivity that can occur with ADHD. ADHD drugs have a seemingly paradoxical effect in that although they are stimulants, they enable the person with ADHD to concentrate better and think more clearly, rather than thinking and acting in a scattered fashion. (Of course these drugs are prescribed at a therapeutic level, and are not taken at the much higher dosage that is taken by the drug abuser to achieve euphoria and other desired effects from abuse.)

Stimulants can also be drugs of abuse and addiction. According to psychiatry professor Steven M. Berman and colleagues, amphetamines are commonly abused prescription medications.[4] Other stimulants, such as methylphenidate, are also used to treat ADHD, and these drugs are also sometimes abused by others. They are most likely to be abused when they are crushed and either taken intranasally ("snorted") or injected. Some abusers dissolve prescribed stimulant tablets in water and inject the mixture, which can be extremely dangerous because of filler materials that were included in the tablets and that can block the blood vessels when injected rather than taken orally as intended.[5]

Most amphetamine abusers are white, and often abusers who misuse prescribed stimulants are college students.[6] In contrast, methamphetamine abusers are often low-income and less-educated whites.[7]

The abuse of illegally made methamphetamine, an analogue of amphetamine that was first synthesized in Japan in 1893[8], is a serious problem in the United States today and it is also one that appears to be on the rise. Methamphetamine acts faster than cocaine and its effects last longer in the body. Consequently, some abusers of cocaine may be switching to this drug of abuse for these reasons. According to the National Institute on Drug Abuse (NIDA), most abused methamphetamine is made illegally in clandestine laboratories in the United States, Mexico, and other countries.[9]

Treatment of amphetamine or methamphetamine abuse is challenging because the individual in a state of withdrawal is often severely depressed, lethargic, and fatigued and cannot pay attention to instructions from therapists or others. The person's former sense of humor is often absent and attempts at joking with the individual are misunderstood, or worse, interpreted as a personal attack, according to therapists. Recovery is possible but requires a great deal of work. Often court-ordered therapy

BLACK BOX WARNINGS FOR AMPHETAMINES

Amphetamines come with "black box" warnings from the Food and Drug Administration, which are warnings inside a bolded black box given to alert consumers to the particular health risks of drugs. Here is the black box warning for Adderall tablets ranging from dosages of 5 mg to 30 mg:

> AMPHETAMINES HAVE A HIGH POTENTIAL FOR ABUSE. ADMINISTRA-TION OF AMPHETAMINES FOR PROLONGED PERIODS OF TIME MAY LEAD TO DRUG DEPENDENCE AND MUST BE AVOIDED. PARTICULAR ATTEN-TION SHOULD BE PAID TO THE POSSIBILITY OF SUBJECTS OBTAINING AMPHETAMINES FOR NONTHERAPEUTIC USE OR DISTRIBUTION TO OTHERS, AND THE DRUGS SHOULD BE PRESCRIBED OR DISPENSED SPARINGLY.
>
> MISUSE OF AMPHETAMINE MAY CAUSE SUDDEN DEATH AND SERIOUS CARDIOVASCULAR ADVERSE EVENTS

works best because the individual is more likely to comply with treatment requirements to avoid going to jail.

WHAT ARE AMPHETAMINES?

Amphetamines are central nervous system stimulants produced by pharmaceutical companies, and these drugs are sometimes diverted to those who abuse them. Methamphetamine, however, can be produced illegally with relative ease.[10] Methamphetamine is a drug that is up to three times more potent than amphetamine and the euphoria lasts hours longer than with amphetamine.[11]

Amphetamines and methylphenidate are also Schedule II stimulants, which are specifically controlled by the federal government, particularly the Drug Enforcement Administration (DEA) as well as the Food and Drug Administration (FDA). Scheduled drugs include some illegal drugs, such as heroin and marijuana, as well as many drugs that are legal but are controlled by the DEA, such as oxycodone, morphine, and amphetamines, as well as other categories of potential drugs of abuse.

Examples of amphetamines are mixed amphetamine salts (Adderall, Adderall XR), dextroamphetamine (Dexedrine), and methamphetamine (Desoxyn). Although prescribed infrequently because of the stigma attached to the word *methamphetamine*, Desoxyn may be prescribed to patients for treating ADHD as well as obesity; however, nearly all researchers are referring to illegal methamphetamine when they make any mention of methamphetamine. According to the DEA, only 14,000 prescriptions for Desoxyn were written in 2009.[12] Note that methylenedioxymethamphetamine—MDMA, which is also known as Ecstasy—is considered an amphetamine-type stimulant by some researchers, but this drug is not addressed in this book because it is a hallucinogenic drug rather than a stimulant.

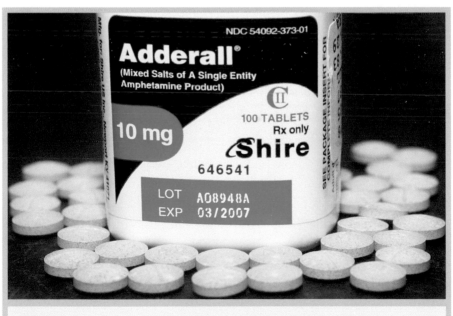

Figure 1.1 Adderall is an amphetamine-based ADHD drug with a high potential for abuse. *(© Getty Images)*

NICKNAMES RELATED TO AMPHETAMINE AND METHAMPHETAMINE

Chalk—methamphetamine

Crystal—A crystallized form of methamphetamine that is smoked

Crank—Smoked crystal methamphetamine

Glass—Smoked crystal methamphetamine

Ice—Smoked crystal methamphetamine

Meth mouth—Extreme tooth decay caused by abuse of methamphetamine

Skippy—Ritalin

The smart drug—Ritalin

Speed—A common name for amphetamine because it stimulates the central nervous system and can make people nervous and agitated or "speeded up"

Tina—Methamphetamine

Uppers—Refers to stimulants that make a person feel energetic, as opposed to "downers" (sedating drugs) that make individuals lethargic and sleepy

GENERAL EFFECTS OF AMPHETAMINES

The effects of amphetamine are long-lasting, extending up to 15 hours after use.[13] Amphetamines are dangerous drugs when abused; for example, amphetamine use and abuse can cause life-threatening hyperthermia (an extremely high body temperature), heart attack, stroke, and other health issues that don't usually happen to young adults—and these health risks can occur on the very first use of the drug as well as with chronic abuse. Psychiatric symptoms such as anxiety, hallucinations, and confusion can also occur with amphetamine abuse. Amphetamine abuse can also cause a psychotic break from reality as well as lead to extremely violent and aggressive or suicidal behavior.[14]

A further complicating factor is that up to 10% of Caucasian individuals have a deficiency in the CYP2D6 enzyme, an enzyme that helps to metabolize both amphetamine and methamphetamine. As a result, these individuals may be more sensitive to the effects of such drugs and they may also be more likely

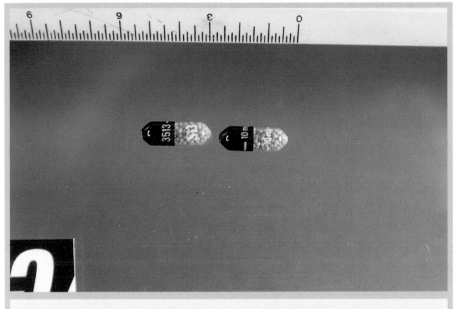

Figure 1.2 Dextroamphetamine (brand name Dexedrine), another central nervous system stimulant, used to treat ADHD. *(U.S. Drug Enforcement Administration)*

to develop complications from their abuse.[15] It is unknown if this enzyme deficiency increases or decreases the risk for the abuse of amphetamines, but further research may be very revealing.

AMPHETAMINE ABUSE AND ADDICTION

According to NIDA, most people who abuse drugs are primarily motivated by one or more of three basic reasons: they want to feel good, they want to feel better, or they want to *do* better. In the case of adolescents, NIDA says, curiosity can be a fourth motivator for the initial abuse of drugs.[16]

If the key motivation is feeling good, the person usually wants to get high, as in feeling euphoric. If they want to feel better than they feel right now, which may be feeling depressed and anxious or experiencing other negative emotions or even physical pain, then they hope that using the illicit drug will make them feel better. Some people wish to perform better, as do some high school and college students who abuse amphetamines to get better grades or athletes who may believe their stamina is increased with amphetamines or other drugs. Of adolescents who abuse drugs for the first time out of curiosity, once they know what using the drug is like, they may continue to use the drug because they want to feel good or better or to perform better.

The risk is that, whatever the initial motivation is in using the drug, if individuals continue to abuse amphetamines, methamphetamine, or methylphenidate, they eventually may become dependent on the drug for their happiness, avoidance of problems, or their ability to succeed. They risk addiction because they believe that the drug gives them what they need better than anything else. And once they become addicted, they need the drug itself, both physically and psychologically, and the initial motivations for taking it become irrelevant. This is why it is important to avoid taking potentially addicting drugs in the first place unless there is a compelling medical reason to take the drug and it is taken under the supervision of a medical doctor. No one is too smart or too rich or too beautiful or too virtuous or too anything else to be safe from the risk of drug dependence once he or she starts taking drugs illegally.

Figure 1.3 Methamphetamine in crystalline form. *(U.S. Drug Enforcement Administration)*

YABA: METHAMPHETAMINE AND CAFFEINE

Yaba is an illegal drug manufactured in Thailand made of methamphetamine and caffeine; the tablets containing these substances are about the size of a pencil eraser. They are often candy flavored and can be taken orally, or they may be melted and the vapors are then inhaled. Yaba appears to be most popular among Asians in California, although there are few known details about its usage. Yaba is also known as "Nazi speed" and "crazy medicine." The same risks that are present with methamphetamine are also present with yaba, including heart attack, stroke, hyperthermia, convulsions, and death. If the drug is injected, users are at risk for contracting the human immunodeficiency virus (HIV) as well as hepatitis and any other blood-borne infections.

DRUG ABUSE DATA

In any discussion of drugs that can be abused, it helps to know the extent to which they are abused. According to the National Survey on Drug Use and Health for 2009 (released in 2010), nearly 22 million Americans used illegal drugs, an increase of 9% from 2008. The number of abusers of methamphetamine increased from 314,000 nationwide in 2008 to 502,000 in 2009, a shocking increase of 60% in just one year. In addition, the number of new users of methamphetamine ages 12 years and older increased from 95,000 in 2008 to 154,000 in 2009.

Illicit drug abuse in general also increased among full-time college students ages 18 to 22 years, from 20.2% in 2008 to 22.7% in 2009. Prescription drug abuse increased as well, from 8% in 2008 to 8.7% in 2009. This is the highest level of prescription drug abuse since 2002. Most prescribed drugs that are abused are painkillers, but other drugs are also abused, such as stimulants. Pamela Hyde, the administrator of the Substance Abuse and Mental Health Services Administration (SAMHSA), says that substance abuse is linked to economic issues, such as the economic slowdown in 2009.[17]

Figure 1.4 One common form of methamphetamine is powder. *(U.S. Drug Enforcement Administration)*

WHY SOME STUDENTS SAY THEY MISUSE ADDERALL

In a study of the motives of 175 college undergraduates who admitted taking amphetamines without a prescription, researchers Alan D. DeSantis and Audrey Curtis Hane performed extensive interviews of the types of excuses that their subjects gave for taking the drugs. The researchers reported on their findings in *Substance Use and Misuse* in 2010.[18]

As seen in the table, for example, some students say that the reason they take the drug is what matters most, and that if they don't take it to get high but instead take it to do well in school, they regard this as a valid reason. Others assume that amphetamines that are made by pharmaceutical companies are automatically safe for everyone. Of course, they are wrong in this assumption, because prescribed drugs should only be given to those who receive a prescription from their physician, a person who has seen them face to face, reviewed their medical history and symptoms, and carefully selected the right medication based on his or her medical training.

Table 1.1 Students' Opinions on Amphetamine Use vs. Reality	
Why Students Say It's Okay to Take Amphetamines Not Prescribed to Them	Why It's Really Not Okay
I'm doing it for the "right" reasons (like doing better on a test). I don't take drugs to get high.	It's illegal to take drugs prescribed to others; the reasons for misusing them are irrelevant. A first-time conviction for selling or giving away amphetamines can be a five-year prison sentence.
Amphetamines are safe when they're made by drug companies, not cooked up by druggies.	Amphetamines are dangerous and a first-time abuse may be fatal.
The FDA approves these drugs so they must be okay for anyone.	The FDA approves amphetamines for individuals who receive a prescription from a doctor.
Prescribed stimulants can't make you high.	They can if you abuse them.
You can't get addicted to ADHD stimulants.	Yes, you can, if you abuse them.
Taking amphetamines without a prescription doesn't hurt me or anyone else.	Amphetamines can harm the heart, brain, and other organs. They also hurt others. In a study of impaired drivers, there was a significant relationship between higher concentrations of amphetamine in the blood and a worse level of traffic impairment, especially in younger drivers.[19]
Taking Adderall is like drinking caffeinated cola or coffee.	Amphetamines are far more dangerous than cola or coffee.
I skip the middleman—the doctor. I think I have ADHD myself.	The doctor is not an optional step to skip if people think they may have ADHD and need ADHD medications.

In another study reported by SAMHSA in 2009, the researchers found that full-time college students ages 18 to 22 were more than twice as likely (6.4%) to have abused the amphetamine Adderall in the past year compared to their noncollege peers (3.0%).[20] This finding was true for both males and females. Of those college students who used Adderall nonmedically, the rate was highest among whites (8.6%), followed by a much lower rate for persons of two or more races (2.7%). Only 1% of African American college students used Adderall nonmedically.

The rates were also high among college students with a family income of less than $20,000 (8.9%), compared with 6.0% of students whose family income was $75,000 or greater.

Table 1.2 Nonmedical Use of Adderall in the Past Year among Full-Time College Students Ages 18 to 22 by Selected Demographic Characteristics	
Demographic Characteristic	Percent
Race/Ethnicity	
White	8.6
Black or African American	1.0
Asian	2.1
Two or More Races	2.7
Hispanic or Latino	2.2
Annual Family Income	
Less than $20,000	8.9
$20,000 to $49,999	3.0
$50,000 to $74,999	4.0
$75,000 or more	6.0

Source: Substance Abuse and Mental Health Services Administration, "Nonmedical Use of Adderall among Full-Time College Students," The NSDUH Report (April 7, 2009). Available online at http://www.oas.samhsa.gov/2k9/adderall/adderall.pdf. Accessed September 10, 2010.

MOST METHAMPHETAMINE ABUSERS ADMITTED FOR TREATMENT ARE WESTERN WHITES

According to the Substance Abuse and Mental Health Services Administration, 65% of methamphetamine abusers who received drug treatment in 2007 were white, followed by 21% who were Hispanic and 5% who were Asian/Pacific Islanders. In addition, most (73% in 2007) resided in the Western part of the United States, followed by 15% in the Midwest, 11% in the South, and only 1% in the Northeast.[21]

METHAMPHETAMINE

Most methamphetamine is used illegally, and it is also a substance that is very addictive. It is a very potent drug, and its effects continue as long as 24 hours beyond the effects of amphetamine.[22] Methamphetamine is a bitter powder that is ingested orally, intranasally, or by injecting the drug or smoking it. Some people insert the drug rectally, as with a suppository.

Some methamphetamine is used lawfully; for example, Desoxyn is a legal form of methamphetamine that can be used to treat ADHD. However, it is very rarely used for this disorder, and instead, most people with ADHD are treated with either amphetamine or methylphenidate, a psychostimulant.

According to a unique analysis of the annual economic cost of methamphetamine in the United States, the RAND Corporation computed a cost of $23.4 billion in 2005, including costs to the criminal justice system, as well as the costs of drug treatment, child welfare, health care, and intangibles such as the premature death of methamphetamine addicts. The researchers also noted that for each pound of methamphetamine that is made illegally, five to six pounds of toxic byproducts are also generated, with potential harm to the health of others in the area and also to the environment.[23]

Illicit methamphetamine is considered relatively simple to make from basic household chemicals. The dangers of making the drug are great—for example, it must be created at very high temperatures—and the dangers of using the drug are enormous. Illegal methamphetamine is very addictive. It is also shockingly aging and disfiguring.

Continued abuse of methamphetamine causes ugly facial and body sores, rotten and black teeth, and an unattractively extreme weight loss. Those are the outside effects that people can see. But the damage is extensive on the inside too, affecting the lungs, heart, kidneys, and virtually every body organ. Psychiatric symptoms include a paranoia that is indistinguishable from paranoid schizophrenia.

Methamphetamine abuse can also cause death, and some people die the very first time that the drug is used. According to Suzanne R. White, M.D., at Wayne State University, in Detroit, individuals have died from ingesting as little as 1.5 mg/kg of methamphetamine, although chronic abusers can use from 5 to 15 grams daily.[24]

Side Effects of Methamphetamine

As with amphetamine abuse, methamphetamine abuse also causes many side effects, such as hyperthermia (a dangerously high body temperature), an increased respiration rate, and increased blood pressure. These effects are also seen with amphetamine, but higher levels of methamphetamine than amphetamine reach the brain, causing it to be more potent than amphetamine, according to NIDA.[25]

Methamphetamine addiction can also lead to hypersexuality and an increased risk for contracting sexually transmitted diseases such as the human immunodeficiency virus (HIV) and hepatitis.

Heavy users also experience physical and social consequences, such as the removal of their children to the child welfare system because of neglect or abuse. When children are exposed to the manufacture of methamphetamine in their homes, they suffer health risks, and some children have died in explosions or fires caused by the very volatile chemicals used in the manufacture of methamphetamine.

Children may not be physically abused when their parents are addicted to methamphetamine, but addicted parents may ignore their children to an extreme level. For example, the methamphetamine user is often not hungry, so it may not occur to him or her to feed the child. Cleanliness is often not important to meth users, so they may fail to bathe small children or change an infant's diapers. As a result, the children are neglected.

Over the long term an individual becomes addicted to methamphetamine, and its effects can include aggressive and even violent behavior, psychosis, and memory loss. Hallucinations often include formication, or the feeling that unseen bugs are crawling on or underneath the skin. Just imagining such a feeling is unpleasant but it is far worse when the person believes it is actually happening. The addict may tear up the skin trying to get rid of these imaginary bugs, which are also known as "**crank bugs**" since they are typical of the experience of methamphetamine addicts.

NIDA says that methamphetamine changes the parts of the brain that control memory and emotion—which is probably why addiction causes memory problems and severe emotional issues.[26] Individuals who abuse methamphetamine may also suffer strokes, and the stroke may be delayed by up to 12 hours after the last use of the drug.[27]

Who Abuses Illicit Methamphetamine

According to research on the use of illegal methamphetamine, published in 2008 by Todd M. Durell and colleagues in *Substance Abuse Treatment, Prevention, and Policy,* in a study of more than 4,000 adults nationwide in the United States ages 18 to 49 years in 2005, 8.6% had ever used methamphetamine. The current abuse rates were less than 1%; for example, less than 1% of all subjects had used the drug in the past year or the past month.

Individuals ages 18 to 25 years had the greatest likelihood of methamphetamine abuse, or 1.79% in the past year. Males were more likely to have ever abused methamphetamine than females—about 10% of males compared to about 7% of females. Education was also a factor. In contrast to prescribed amphetamine abusers who included many college students, when it came to methamphetamine abuse, the results were very different. Individuals without a high school diploma were four times more likely to have ever used methamphetamine (about 21%) than college graduates (about 5%).[28]

Table 1.3 Prevalence of Nonmedical Methamphetamine Use by Demographic Characteristics, Percentage				
	Lifetime	Past 3 Years	Past Year	Past Month
Overall	8.63	2.13	0.71	0.27
Age				
18–25	6.04	3.63	1.79	0.60
26–49	9.46	1.65	0.36	0.17
Gender				
Male	10.03	3.14	0.86	0.32
Female	7.27	1.14	0.56	0.23
Education				
Less than high school	20.64	4.40	0.25	0.02
High school graduate	6.12	1.34	0.80	0.21
Some college	7.31	2.34	0.67	0.31
College graduate	5.31	1.41	0.95	0.47

Source: Todd M. Durell, et al., "Prevalence of Nonmedical Methamphetamine Use in the United States," *Substance Abuse Treatment, Prevention, and Policy*, p. 4. Available online at http://www.substanceabuse policy.com/content/3/1/19. Accessed September 10, 2010. Copyright 2008 by Biomed Central Ltd. Reproduced with permission of Biomed Central Ltd. in the format Tradebook via Copyright Clearance Center.

CONSIDERING METHYLPHENIDATE

Another stimulant that is sometimes misused or abused is methylphenidate (Ritalin), a drug with a chemical structure that is similar to amphetamine. It is often prescribed to treat children, adolescents, and adults with ADHD. If abused at high dosages, however, its effects are similar to the effects of amphetamines.[29] Note that Concerta is also a form of methylphenidate, but is believed to be much more difficult to abuse than short-acting drugs such as Ritalin.[30]

Table 1.4 ADHD Medications Approved by the FDA		
Trade Name	**Generic Name**	**Approved Age***
Adderall	Amphetamine	3 and older
Adderall XR	Amphetamine (extended release)	6 and older
Concerta	Methylphenidate (long acting)	6 and older
Daytrana	Methylphenidate skin patch	6 and older
Desoxyn	Methamphetamine hydrochloride	6 and older
Dexedrine	Dextroamphetamine	3 and older
Dextrostat	Dextroamphetamine	3 and older
Focalin	Dexmethylphenidate	6 and older
Focalin XR	Dexmethylphenidate (extended release)	6 and older
Metadate CD	Methylphenidate (extended release capsule)	6 and older
Metadate ER	Methylphenidate (extended release tablet)	6 and older
Methylin	Methylphenidate (oral solution and chewable tablets)	6 and older
Ritalin	Methylphenidate	6 and older
Ritalin LA	Methylphenidate (long acting)	6 and older
Ritalin SR	Methylphenidate (extended release)	6 and older
Strattera**	Atomoxetine	6 and older
Vyvanse	Lisdexamfetamine dimesylate	6 and older

*Not all ADHD medications are approved for use in adults with ADHD.
**Strattera is not a stimulant drug. All other drugs in the table are central nervous system stimulants.
Note: ER ("extended release") means that the medication is released gradually so that a controlled amount enters the body over a period of time. LA ("long acting") means the medication stays in the body for a long time.
Source: National Institute of Mental Health, *Attention Deficit Hyperactivity Disorder*, p. 8. Available online at http://www.nimh.nih.gov/health/publications/attention-deficit-hyperactivity-disorder/adhd_booklet.pdf. Accessed December 1, 2010.

One problem that has been identified with some individuals with ADHD is that they are willing to give away or sell their medication to others, and they can often find others who are eager to try the drug. In a study of 66 adults ages 18 years and older (with an average age of 27.0 years) who were prescribed methylphenidate, the researchers found that 29% admitted to using their own medications inappropriately and 44% admitted to diverting their drugs to others—with the overwhelming majority of those who diverted the drug giving their medications to others rather than selling them.[31]

Of those who misused their medication while taking other substances, most (89%) misused their medication while they were taking other drugs. Of this group, 92% took their medication along with alcohol, while 77% took the drug with cannabis (marijuana), and 31% took it with cocaine. The researchers also found that misusers were more likely to have a past history of substance abuse with the hallucinogenic drug psilocybin (73.7%) compared to non-misusers (31.9%) as well as with the abuse of cocaine (57.9% for misusers compared with 19.1% for non-misusers) and amphetamines (52.6% for misusers compared with 14.9% for non-misusers). Misusers of their medication were also more likely to divert their medications to others than non-misusers.

Diversion of their medication to others was associated with age, with younger individuals and individuals prescribed their methylphenidate at younger ages being at higher risk for diversion. In contrast, compliance with taking their medication was higher among those individuals who attended an ADHD support group.[32]

2
Historical Background

It was 1937 and Wanda, age 25, was having really bad periods. She also felt sluggish and sad all the time. Wanda consulted her doctor and he said he had the perfect medication for her: Benzedrine. It was a drug he said would make her feel much more energetic and happy and also help her experience less pain during her monthly cycles. So Wanda began taking the Benzedrine tablets. After a while, the dosage the doctor recommended didn't work that well for her, so she started taking more. And then even more. It was easy to get at the drugstore, since no prescription was required. Wanda became addicted to the drug and eventually, she reluctantly told the doctor that she was always thinking about and needing her Benzedrine. He became curt and said that was impossible, that nobody needed large amounts of amphetamines. There must be something really wrong with Wanda—maybe she needed to see a psychiatrist.

Amphetamines, including methamphetamine, have been available for nearly a hundred years, helping some people with problems such as narcolepsy—sudden and uncontrollable lapses of sleep that can be averted with amphetamine. These drugs have also been addicting individuals for about the same length of time, although for many years amphetamines were perceived as wonder drugs that could cure just about anything, ranging from depression[1] and schizophrenia[2] to dysmenorrhea[3] (difficult menstrual periods) and other ailments. Starting in the twentieth century and continuing to the present, amphetamines have been used to treat children, adolescents, and adults with ADHD.

THE ORIGINS OF AMPHETAMINES

Ephedrine, a component of many cold medications sold today, is the precursor of both amphetamine and methamphetamine. According to researchers Ralph Weisheit and William L. White in their book *Methamphetamine: Its History, Pharmacology, and Treatment,* ephedrine was first synthesized by chemist

MEDICAL PROBLEMS FOR WHICH AMPHETAMINES WERE USED IN THE EARLY TO MID-TWENTIETH CENTURY

- Alcoholism
- Allergies
- Asthma
- Bedwetting
- Chronic hiccups
- Depression
- Hyperactivity in children
- Low sexual libido
- Menstrual problems
- Morphine addiction
- Obesity
- Schizophrenia
- Seasickness
- Smoking cessation

Sources: Charles O. Jackson, "The Amphetamine Inhaler: A Case Study of Medical Abuse," *Journal of the History of Medicine* 26 (1971): 187–196; Nicolas Rasmussen, *On Speed: The Many Lives of Amphetamine.* New York: New York University Press, 2008; Ralph Weisheit, and William L. White, *Methamphetamine: Its History, Pharmacology, and Treatment.* Center City, Minn.: Hazelden, 2009; Mark Rose, "Methamphetamine Abuse and Dependence," Continuing Medical Education Resource (Sacramento, Calif.), at http://www.netce.com/492/Course_5181.pdf (accessed December 1, 2010); E. Davidoff G. L. Goodstone, "Amphetamine Barbiturate Therapy in Psychiatric Conditions," *Psychiatric Quarterly* 16 (1942): p. 541; W. B. Brown, "Benzedrine Sulfate in Dysmenorrhea," *Missouri State Medical Association Journal* 39 (1942): 253; S. W. Kalb, "Observation on 1,200 Cases of Obesity Treated with Amphetamine (Benzedrine) Sulfate," *New Jersey Medical Society Journal* 40 (1943): 385–387.

Lazăr Edeleanu in 1887 at the University of Berlin, while methamphetamine was first synthesized by Japanese pharmacologist Nagayoshi Nagai in 1893.[4]

In 1929, Southern California biochemist Gordon Alles developed the formula for phenylisopropylamine, later known as amphetamine. He was actively seeking to create a new decongestant[5] that would be a pharmaceutical hit. After the introduction of the Benzedrine inhaler in 1933,[6] amphetamine became a more popular drug than Alles could ever have imagined, and amphetamine was used for a startling number of ailments, as listed in the sidebar. Benzedrine was also introduced as a tablet in 1938, after receiving approval from the American Medical Association in late 1937 for this use. In fact, the medical profession actively embraced Benzedrine.

The Philadelphia pharmaceutical firm of Smith, Kline and French introduced the Benzedrine inhaler in 1933 for people with nasal congestion and asthma.[7] However, the public quickly learned that the product caused sleeplessness, and as a result, it became popular with students pulling all-nighters to study for exams at the last minute. Once others learned about its full abuse potential, it became popular with many people, such as prisoners (for whom inhaler strips were smuggled to them in letters) and others seeking a euphoric high.[8] According to Charles Jackson in his article on the amphetamine inhaler, one inmate in an Army prison was found to have more than 300 empty inhalers in his possession.[9]

THE BENZEDRINE INHALER

The FDA began requiring prescriptions for amphetamines subsequent to the 1938 Food, Drug and Cosmetic Act, but the Benzedrine inhaler was not covered under the federal statutes interpreted by the FDA. It became apparent that some individuals were abusing the drug by cracking open the inhaler and eating the amphetamine-soaked cotton strips inside, gaining an instant high, based on complaints that the FDA had received. The product was a hard container containing eight strips impregnated with 250 mgs of amphetamine, which equaled the dosage from about 25 Benzedrine tablets that were 10 mg each.[10]

Smith, Kline and French and other drug companies made the amphetamine inhalers. Smith, Kline and French had a patent on one form of amphetamine but other companies developed different formulations. Most companies tried to deter the abuse of their products, by introducing nausea-inducing agents for individuals who ate the amphetamine extracted from the inhalers. They also made the product foul-tasting if ingested rather than taken nasally. Abusers toughed out the nausea for the euphoria that they knew was coming. They also got around the bad taste by dumping the product in carbonated drinks or wine. In addition, manufacturers tried hardening the containers so that they would be very difficult to break open. That didn't work. People who were determined to abuse the drugs found ways to break into the containers.

STIMULANTS AND THEIR USE IN TREATING ADHD

In 1902, British pediatrician Sir George Still, a professor of childhood disease at King's College Hospital in London, gave several lectures on children with excessive restlessness who were oppositional and failed to respond to punishment, also stating that there were sub-groups of hyperactive behavior. Later research built on Still's initial findings.[11]

In 1937, Rhode Island physician Charles Bradley was a psychiatrist at the Bradley Home. Launched by his granduncle, the Bradley Home was a facility for children with severe health problems. At the point of admission to the home, some of the children were given a painful spinal tap, which caused the children to subsequently complain of severe headaches. Bradley decided to try Benzedrine on 30 children to relieve these induced headaches, and he accidentally discovered the drug was effective in the treatment of hyperactive children, greatly improving both their behavior and academic performance. Bradley also found that when he took the children off Benzedrine, their prob-lem behavior returned. Bradley's discovery ultimately led to the use of stimulants for the treatment of children and adolescents with ADHD several decades later.[12]

During this time, physicians believed that the problem of children with hyperactivity and impulsivity likely lay in brain damage. In the 1950s, the disorder was called hyperkinetic impulse disorder and it

Because of continued complaints of abuse, Smith, Kline and French voluntarily removed the Benzedrine inhaler from the market in 1949. But this did not end the inhaler abuse nor did it end amphetamine abuse. By 1953, the FDA again began receiving numerous complaints of abuse with other amphetamine inhalers. Finally, in 1959, the FDA announced that the amphetamine inhaler would no longer be sold as an over-the-counter drug and it would available by prescription only. This effectively ended the abuse of many amphetamine inhalers, although some companies continued to produce them even after the

was later referred to as minimal brain disorder. In later years, physicians were skeptical that children with these behaviors had any brain damage.

In 1972, Canadian physician Virginia Douglas at McGill University renamed the condition attention deficit disorder, both with and without hyperactivity, in the *Diagnostic and Statistical Manual III* published by the American Psychiatric Association. The DSM and its definition of ADHD were further revised in 1987 and again in 2000, and a current revision is in process as of this writing.[13]

In the mid-1970s and again in the 1990s, there were two separate backlashes against the use of stimulants to treat children, and some opponents speculated that the drug was dangerous and overprescribed, as well as abused.[14]

Today, children, adolescents, and adults with symptoms of impulsivity, inattentiveness, and lack of concentration, and sometimes hyperactivity, may be diagnosed with ADHD. The first choice of the drug used to treat ADHD is a stimulant. If a stimulant is not indicated for some reason, then physicians may consider atomoxetine (Strattera), a non-stimulant drug.[15]

One paradox of the general acceptance of the use of amphetamines for individuals with ADHD, however, is that it may generate a widespread belief that such drugs are inherently safe, which then serves to undermine the public perception that amphetamines should be avoided because of their danger.

ban went into effect; for example, the Wyamine inhaler included an amphet-aminelike drug, and it was not withdrawn from the market until 1971.[16]

ABUSE OF ORAL AMPHETAMINES

Celebrities such as authors Tennessee Williams and Truman Capote and sing-ers such as Eddie Fisher were abusers of amphetamines. But average people also used the drugs. For example, in a 1967 issue of *Good Housekeeping* mag-azine, a housewife described how she started taking amphetamines to lose weight after a pregnancy on the advice of her doctor. She used the drugs daily for five years and she ultimately had to be hospitalized for gastroenteritis. It was then that she went through a painful withdrawal from amphetamines, a drug she didn't know that she was addicted to. She said, "Well, you hear about drug addicts climbing the walls when they need a fix. I know now what *that* means. I couldn't sit or lie down. I paced the floor, shaking. My head felt like it was separating from my body, just floating. Next morning, when Dave [her husband] took me home, I thought I was flying apart. I went straight for my bottle and took a pill. Half an hour later, I was 'normal' again. And then I knew for sure. I was hooked, as surely as if I'd been on heroin." She then called the pharmacy and found out what was in her pills: Dexedrine, an amphet-amine, and Compazine, a tranquilizer and antipsychotic.[17]

METHAMPHETAMINE AND ITS ORIGINS

Methamphetamine was commonly used in the United States and Europe in the mid-twentieth century. For example, some doctors treated cocaine and heroin addiction with injections of Methedrine, the brand name of a former drug containing methamphetamine.[18]

Methamphetamine also became a popular drug among many famous people in the United States and other countries. It is now believed, for exam-ple, that President John F. Kennedy used injections of methamphetamine to control the fatigue and pain from his severe health problems, including a back injury and Addison's disease, a serious endocrine disorder.[19] Accord-ing to researcher Nicolas Rasmussen, other regular users received injections from Manhattan physician Max Jacobson (1900–1979), also known as "Dr. Feelgood," including such late luminaries as Congressman Claude Pep-per of Florida, film producer and director Cecil B. DeMille, and Tennessee

CRYSTAL METH

Crystal methamphetamine, or crystal meth, is a crystalline form of methamphetamine that can be smoked or injected. In the latter part of the 1970s and early 1980s, motorcycle gangs in California, such as the Hells Angels, were the initial means of proliferation of crystal meth, which is supposedly the reason why the drug is also called **"crank,"** since it was hidden in the crankcase of motorcycles. The drug first took off in the western part of the country, in California, Colorado, and other states, including Hawaii. However, individuals throughout the country quickly learned that there was a demand for crystal methamphetamine and that it is not difficult to make. It is synthesized from ephedrine or pseudoephedrine and some "recipes" are readily available on the Internet.

Of course, what proponents do not mention is that the illegal manufacture of methamphetamine is a highly volatile and explosive process, and people have been injured or killed while making this drug. In addition, both they and their children can be affected by the noxious fumes created in the process of making the drug.

There is also a mythology surrounding crystal meth that indicates that it is a drug far more powerful than other forms of methamphetamine. However, according to DEA experts, these myths are generally purveyed by drug dealers. DEA experts report that in contrast to crack cocaine, which is much more rapidly addicting than is powdered cocaine, crystalline methamphetamine is not more addictive than powdered methamphetamine.[21] However, all forms of illegal methamphetamine have a high risk for addiction.

Williams.[20] This form of methamphetamine was used legally by people in past years.

WORLD WAR II AND AMPHETAMINES

No discussion of amphetamines and methamphetamine would be complete without a look at the proliferation of the use of these drugs by military individuals—mostly men, because mostly men fought during World War II, including Americans as well as the British, Germans, Japanese, and military men from other countries. Military leaders believed that these drugs would give their fighting forces an extra edge, enabling them to survive the ordeals of combat, which is often comprised of long periods of boredom punctuated by terrifying times of hard and life-threatening combat.

In the United States, the drug of choice for soldiers, sailors, and airmen was the Benzedrine tablet, issued in emergency medical kits, survival kits, and aviation packs as 5 mg pills. The British also used amphetamine during the war, and according to author Nicolas Rasmussen, 72 million tablets of Benzedrine were used by the British military, primarily by those in combat.[22] In contrast, the Japanese and German military members were issued methamphetamine tablets. Rasmussen believed that the issuance of such tablets created an environment of abuse that carried over into civilian life. He noted that in a 1945 military prison population, nearly a third of the abusers had begun abusing Benzedrine while in the military. Says Rasmussen, "Twenty-seven percent of [the imprisoned] abusers had been given amphetamine during military service, mainly by an officer, and in tablet form, compared with 5% of nonabusers—an odds ratio of 7.0. There is thus strong evidence that Benzedrine abuse, although an existing practice, was multiplied many times by military exposure, at least among vulnerable subpopulations. And although these prisoners were not typical of military personnel, neither, in the judgment of the psychiatrists, were most of them particularly abnormal young men."[23]

In wartime Germany, soldiers were issued methamphetamine, known at the time as Pervitin. Says Rasmussen, "Authorities were already aware that the drug was being used by some soldiers, who were obtaining it on their own. Nevertheless, they officially listed Pervitin (in 3 mg tablets) among the medicines that physicians in military units could requisition in 1939—just in time for the campaign that crushed Poland. In the Blitzkrieg's opening months, German troops were widely issued the drug. Pervitin proved popular among Hitler's fighting men: the German military consumed 35 million methamphetamine tablets in April, May, and June 1940, the peak season of the Blitz. There were no orders from Berlin to use it in any particular way, so this consumption reflects demand among the soldiers and medics at the front."[24]

Rasmussen also noted that in 1941 the German government placed both amphetamine and methamphetamine under narcotics regulation, available only with a special prescription and consumption subsequently dropped significantly. Interestingly, this was nearly 30 years before these drugs were acknowledged as dangerous in the United States.

According to a report from the United Nations, the Japanese people experienced a methamphetamine abuse epidemic subsequent to World War II, related to the hoarding of the drug during wartime, leaving many drugs available.[25] At that time, the population of the entire country was about 89 million, and an estimated 2 million people were abusing methamphetamine from about 1945 to 1955.[26] This abuse ended in 1955 after a major effort against such abuse by the Japanese government.

AMPHETAMINE SALES IN THE SIXTIES AND SEVENTIES

Although most Benzedrine inhalers were gone by the 1960s, and amphetamines were available by prescription only, amphetamine production was still high. According to Rasmussen, in 1962, annual production of amphetamines was 80,000 kg or the equivalent of 43 doses of 10 mg each per year for each person living in the United States at that time. He says, "Thus, in amphetamine alone, the United States in the early 1960s was using nearly as much psychotropic medication as the 65 doses per person per year in the present decade that social critics today find so extraordinary."[27]

The drug also proved to be popular among athletes; for example, Danish cyclist Knut Jensen died of an amphetamine overdose during the 1960 Summer Olympics. There was also a flourishing black market of amphetamines in the late 1960s and early 1970s. For example, according to authors Lester Grinspoon and Peter Hedblom, of 12 billion amphetamine tablets produced in 1971, about half these drugs were diverted to the black market.[28]

Depression and Anxiety

Amphetamines were heavily marketed for mild depression in the mid-twentieth century, and some authors believe that they were the first drugs marketed for depression.[29] Author Rasmussen noted that in 1936, neurologist Abraham Myerson, who coined the term "**anhedonia**" to denote an absence of the ability to feel pleasure or interest in sex, sleep, or food accompanied by a low level of energy, was an advocate for amphetamines, especially Benzedrine, as a restorative for energy, concentration, and pleasure.[30]

Amphetamines were also marketed for anxiety.[31] Patients with so-called somatic symptoms such as fatigue were also prescribed amphetamines. (Somatic symptoms are vague symptoms, such as general fatigue, for which it is often hard for the doctor to determine the cause, let alone the treatment.) Many people who are depressed are tired, however, and amphetamines can improve that symptom. The problem with amphetamines, however, is that too high of a dosage for too long can lead to serious symptoms, such as **amphetamine toxicity**, which induces severe psychiatric symptoms.

Diet Drugs

Amphetamines have been popular as diet drugs since the 1940s when Desoxyn and Hydrin were approved for the treatment of obesity by the FDA. This popularity was further supported and escalated because of a medical journal article on "The Obese Patient," published in 1947, in which a doctor reported that 100 patients lost as much as 28 pounds in 90 days after taking amphetamine. The doctor did not tell the individuals that he was giving them amphetamines and they had other health problems; for example, 74% suffered from fatigue and 59% suffered from nervousness. The individuals allegedly experienced no increases in their blood pressure, according to the doctor.[32]

Dexedrine (dextroamphetamine) was a popular drug prescribed for weight loss and depression. Note that many obese people are also depressed, so this drug may have seemed like a dream drug for individuals with both symptoms. Amphetamines became increasingly popular for weight loss in the 1950s and beyond.

An estimated one-third of all amphetamines prescribed in 1960 were given for weight loss while the rest were given for depression and anxiety as well as for vague complaints. Rasmussen says 85% of amphetamine patients were females and most were ages 36 to 45 years. Many were taking Dexamyl, a product that combined amphetamine with amobarbital, a barbiturate drug, to make for a less jittery patient, although some took Desbutal, a drug that combined methamphetamine with pentobarbital or they took Ambar, a combination of methamphetamine and phenobarbital.[33]

Rasmussen says some diet doctors made huge profits from the amphetamines they sold directly to patients in the 1960s, and noted that one doctor paid $71 for 100,000 amphetamine tablets, which he then sold for $12,000.[34]

In 1972, the FDA announced the findings of their Amphetamine Anorectic Drug Project, which covered 10,000 subjects involved in 200 weight loss

A TOTAL WAR ON DRUGS

It was President Richard Nixon, elected in 1968, who first declared a "total war" on drugs, which culminated in his convincing Congress to pass the Comprehensive Drug Abuse Prevention and Control Act of 1970. This act created a new agency in 1973, the Drug Enforcement Administration.[36] In 1986, President Ronald Reagan signed the Omnibus Anti-Drug Abuse Act of 1986, which increased criminal penalties for drug offenders, concentrating heavily on the abuse of heroin and cocaine. However, amphetamines were scheduled as controlled drugs, as was methylphenidate.

studies using amphetamines and related drugs. According to Eric Colman, M.D., in his article on the history of anorectics, the meta-analysis showed most patients lost only about a pound a week; however, it was a statistically significant study, so the FDA decided amphetamines and similar drugs were effective for the treatment of obesity and approved them for that purpose.[35]

LAWS AFFECTING AMPHETAMINE USE

In 1970, concerned about the abuse of drugs in the United States, Congress passed the Comprehensive Drug Abuse Prevention and Control Act (often referred to as the Controlled Substances Act), a law that created the scheduling of specific drugs into five separate categories, from Schedule I, which comprised illegal drugs such as marijuana and heroin, to Schedule V, which included cough syrups with codeine. Amphetamines and methamphetamine were categorized as Schedule II drugs, as was methylphenidate. Doctors may prescribe drugs under this category but they may not order refills. A new prescription must be written for each 30-day use of the drug. Drugs that are categorized as Schedule III through Schedule V, in contrast, may be prescribed with refills.

The new law also created the Drug Enforcement Administration, an organization that was given national law enforcement powers stemming from the act. In the 1990s, Congress became particularly concerned about the abuse of illegally manufactured methamphetamine and in 1996, the Comprehensive Methamphetamine Control Act was signed into law, which increased the penalties for manufacturing and selling methamphetamine.[37]

Concern over methamphetamine persisted and in 2005, the Combat Methamphetamine Epidemic Act was passed. The law compels retailers to keep chemicals that could be used to make methamphetamine in locked cabinets or behind store counters.[38]

THE PRESENT

Researcher Rasmussen says the first amphetamine epidemic was created by the drug industry and by mostly well-meaning prescribers of amphetamines. Rasmussen believes that there is an epidemic of amphetamine abuse in the United States today. He says the key difference between the first wave of amphetamine abuse in the twentieth century was that it was largely iatrogenic, which means that it was given to treat problems that people did not have or problems with which the drug could not help them; consequently, the drug itself created problems of abuse and dependence. He alleges that today's "epidemic" is due to an increased supply of amphetamines in the drug pipeline along with people choosing to abuse them. Yet Rasmussen admits that studies show that when stimulants are taken as directed to treat ADHD, this usage apparently does not show that individuals with ADHD have a predisposition toward abuse or dependence.[39] Says Rasmussen,

> Other than converting attention deficit disorder patients into abusers, prescribed amphetamines can contribute to the national stimulant epidemic in at least 2 other ways. For one, the mere distribution of so many stimulant tablets in the population creates a hazard. Diversion from students with attention deficit prescriptions to those without is known to occur in high schools, and at American universities, both diversion and nonmedical use by those with prescriptions are commonplace. In 2005, some 600,000 Americans used psychiatric stimulants other than methamphetamine nonmedically in the past month. Thus, legally manufactured attention deficit medications like

Adderall and Ritalin appear to be supplying frequent, and not just casual, misusers.[40]

It also may be true that the current active move against illicit methamphetamine should also include actions against illicit abusers of prescribed amphetamines. It is possible there may be a class issue that is present: Most abusers of methamphetamine are low-income and uneducated individuals, while abusers of prescribed amphetamines are more likely to be educated and higher income individuals. Yet society needs to ask itself if it is reasonable to move actively against methamphetamine alone, with its admittedly dire consequences of abuse and dependence, and yet look the other way when prescribed amphetamines are misused and abused.

It is also true that there is a sort of "generational forgetting" that occurs through time, and the current generation may need to relearn the lessons of history—or, to paraphrase George Santyana, "Those who cannot learn from the mistakes of the past with regard to amphetamines are condemned to repeat them."

3

How Amphetamines Work in the Body

Alice was addicted to methamphetamine. She woke up thinking about it—when she did sleep, which wasn't too often—and she thought about methamphetamine as she planned how to obtain more. When she was using the drug, she didn't think about it, because she reveled in its euphoric effects, until they wore off again. Then she started plotting and planning all over again on where and how to get more meth. Alice had sold everything she owned and was now staying with some other meth addicts in an abandoned building on the outskirts of town. She'd done some sex for drugs and would do more if she had to because the only thing that mattered to her now was to get the drug and use it. Alice was 22 years old but she looked a lot more like she was 50, if she looked in the mirror. Which she didn't do much anymore.

Amphetamine (and to an even greater extent, methamphetamine) directly affects the brain by stimulating the production of high levels of dopamine in the body. Dopamine is a brain chemical that increases pleasure in the brain. How fast the ingested drug affects the person depends on which drug is used and how it is used. For example, if methamphetamine is smoked, it takes effect within 10 seconds, and if it is injected, its effects occur in about 30 seconds, according to Perry N. Halkitis, a professor at New York University and the author of *Methamphetamine Addiction*. If the drug is inhaled (also referred to as "snorting"), the effects occur within up to five minutes.[1] The oral administration of the drug takes the longest to affect the user, or up to 30 minutes. As may be expected, smoking and injecting are the most popular means of use among abusers and addicts. Both amphetamine and methamphetamine can lead to increased wakefulness, decreased appetite, irregular heartbeat, elevated blood pressure, and hyperthermia (high body temperature).[2]

Amphetamines can also be administered rectally, which is the choice of some gay males. In general, they may be placed into a suppository before insertion, although the means of insertion may vary with the individual.

The long-term abuse of methamphetamine can include extreme weight loss, major dental problems, insomnia, confusion, and even violent behavior.[3]

According to addiction expert Carlton K. Erickson, some people who become addicted to drugs report that they felt like a "switch" was turned on when they lost all control of their addiction, while other addicts report that during treatment and recovery they felt like the switch was turned off when they regained control.[4]

THE PROCESS OF ADDICTION

The first step toward addiction is taking an addictive drug. Of course, not everyone who takes drugs becomes an addict. But the risk can be entirely avoided by not using an addictive drug even once. Addiction includes both a psychological and a physical component. The psychological component refers to the person's feeling that they not only need a substance but they also *must* have the substance. The addicted person centers his or her life around acquiring and using the drug, and other aspects of life are of much lower importance, whether it is a job, the family, or their own health.

There is also a physical aspect to addiction in that the body builds up a **tolerance** to the substance, such that greater amounts of amphetamine or methamphetamine are needed to achieve the same feelings of euphoria and well-being. In addition, if the person does not use the addictive drug, whether it is because they cannot or choose to not use it, then he or she feels bad. In the case of stimulants such as amphetamine and methamphetamine, not using the drug often causes anhedonia, or an inability to experience any pleasure at all. This emotional flatness is in very sharp contrast to the major highs that the stimulant provides.

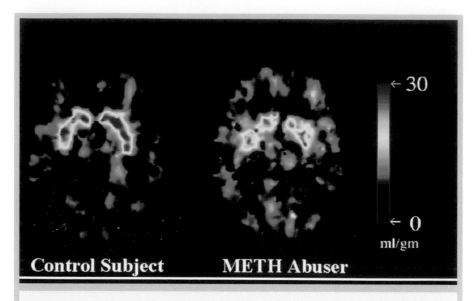

Figure 3.1 Methamphetamine users experience higher levels of dopamine in their brains, but when methamphetamine use is stopped, they often experience a decrease below normal levels. (© *Visuals Unlimited*)

Some people continue using stimulants or they return to stimulant abuse after going off them because they feel they can never experience any pleasure again without the use of drugs. They are wrong. Although they will not feel the euphoric highs associated with stimulant abuse, the anhedonia is a temporary problem and eventually normal feelings of pleasure will be experienced again by the former abuser who stops taking drugs.

SIGNS OF ACUTE AND CHRONIC METHAMPHETAMINE USE

There are signs and symptoms of acute methamphetamine use as well as chronic use. For example, a user who has taken a high dose of methamphetamine may experience such favorable psychological symptoms as increased confidence and boosted self-esteem as well as sexual arousal. However, the person may experience psychosis, paranoia, or hallucinations. He or she may also experience many physiological symptoms, such as an elevated body temperature (hyperthermia), increased heart rate, and profuse sweating.

Behavioral symptoms may include restlessness, aggressive behavior, and perseveration, which is the repeated performance of a meaningless task.

The chronic methamphetamine abuser, as seen in Table 3.2, may experience persistent anxiety, homicidal or suicidal thinking, insomnia, and delusions and hallucinations. There are many physiological signs of abuse, such as high blood pressure, hair loss, malnutrition, and nosebleeds.

Table 3.1 Signs and Symptoms of Acute Methamphetamine Use	
Psychological Symptoms	Increased confidence and self-esteem Grandiosity Feeling of well-being Heightened attentiveness Sexual arousal Paranoia Psychosis Hallucinations, including delusions of parasitosis (a belief one is infected with parasites) Depression Acute anxiety Unprovoked aggressive/violent behavior Irritability
Physiological Signs	Increased heart rate Elevated body temperature Insomnia Increased blood pressure Increased respiration rate Profuse sweating Tremors Neurological symptoms, such as headaches Vision loss
Behavioral Signs	Excessive talkativeness Excitation Agitation Aggressive behavior Uncontrollable jaw clenching Restlessness Performance of repetitive, meaningless tasks
Source: Mark Rose, *Methamphetamine Abuse and Dependence*. A CME Resource. Sacramento, Calif., 2010, p. 9. Available online at http://www.netce.com/492/Course_5181.pdf. Accessed December 1, 2010. Reprinted from Mark Rose, *Methamphetamine Abuse and Dependence*. Sacramento, Calif.: CME Resource. Copyright 2008; used with permission from CME Resource.	

Table 3.2 Signs and Symptoms of Chronic Methamphetamine Use	
Psychological Symptoms	Persistent anxiety Paranoia Insomnia Auditory hallucinations Delusions Psychotic or violent behavior Homicidal or suicidal thinking
Physiological Signs	High blood pressure Pronounced fatigue Malnutrition Neglected hygiene Hair loss Cardiovascular and renal (kidney) damage from toxic by-products of methamphetamine production Choreoathetoid (involuntary movement) disorders Sexual dysfunction Cerebrovascular damage Weight loss (possibly substantial) Nosebleed from intranasal ingestion Dental problems, such as cracked teeth Muscle cramping from dehydration and depleted electrolytes Dermatitis around the mouth from smoking Smell of stale urine stemming from ammonia (a manufacturing component) Dermatological conditions, such as excoriated skin lesions Constipation from dehydration and lack of dietary fiber Dyspnea and coughing up blood from smoking
Behavioral Signs	Unprovoked violent behavior Poor coping abilities Disorganized lifestyle Unemployment Relationship estrangement

Source: Mark Rose, *Methamphetamine Abuse and Dependence*. A CME Resource. Sacramento, Calif., 2010, p. 10. Available online at http://www.netce.com/492/Course_5181.pdf. Accessed December 1, 2010.
Reprinted from Mark Rose, *Methamphetamine Abuse and Dependence*. Sacramento, Calif.: CME Resource. Copyright 2008; used with permission from CME Resource.

A HIGHER SENSITIVITY TO AMPHETAMINES MAY INCREASE ABUSE RISK

Some research indicates that some individuals, particularly those who are high sensation seekers, may be more likely to become abusers of amphetamines. In general, sensation seekers are those who seek out new and novel experiences that they perceive as exciting.

In a small study of 10 high sensation seekers and ten low sensation seekers (those who scored high or low on a test on impulsive sensation-seeking), all adults were given dextroamphetamine. In later sessions, the subjects were given the chance to work for a dose of the drug as a reward. The researchers found that the high sensation seekers were more likely to want to work for the drug. They were also significantly more sensitive to the effect of the drug than the low sensation seekers in that they had a significantly greater self-rated cardiovascular response than was reported by the low sensation seekers.[5]

The researchers hypothesized that being a high sensation seeker increases the likelihood of using drugs and further, the increased sensitivity of the high sensation seekers to the drug puts them at greater risk for drug dependence. That is, they are more likely to try the drug and to like it than are low sensation seekers.

AMPHETAMINE TOXICITY

Amphetamine toxicity, also known as amphetamine overdose, can occur with any form of amphetamine or methamphetamine. This condition refers to dangerously high levels of the drug in the body that can lead to adverse consequences, such as rhabdomyolysis. This is a breakdown of muscle fibers that are released into the bloodstream and can cause kidney failure. Heart attack or stroke can stem from amphetamine toxicity, as can psychosis. The person may also develop respiratory depression. Normally stimulants increase the respiration rate but in an overdose state, they can decrease it.[6]

The person with amphetamine toxicity needs urgent medical attention. Physicians may administer benzodiazepine drugs to calm the patient. Hyperthermic patients may be given ice packs to bring down their body temperature. Patients with cardiac symptoms may require heart medications and even defibrillation.[7]

VIOLENCE AND METHAMPHETAMINE

Some methamphetamine users and addicts become physically violent, and there are several key mechanisms for such violence. For example, the drug may cause psychosis and cause the individual to become violent when he or she would not normally exhibit violence. The drug may also be used to rationalize or explain away acts of violence that are not truly caused by use of the drug.

Methamphetamine abuse may also escalate violence in a person who is prone to violent acts but who can normally suppress such impulses. In addition, the drug can escalate the level of violence among individuals with troubled pasts, such as those who were abused as children.[8]

According to Weisheit and White in their book on methamphetamine, the major factors in the link between violence and methamphetamine are social isolation, paranoia, preexisting aggressive tendencies, a culture that accepts the use of drugs, the use of large doses of methamphetamine, and the use of other drugs in addition to methamphetamine.[9]

Some researchers have devised other theories to explain the presence of violent behavior among drug users. For example, two researchers, Sharon M. Boles and Karen Miotto, provide three justifications for drug use and violence, including what they refer to as *psychopharmacological violence,* or violence that stems from the use of the drug and that causes irritability, paranoia, and excitability. They see *systemic violence* as violent behavior that occurs among drug dealers, such as those dealing with the police, rival gangs, and so forth. *Economic compulsive violence* is their explanation for violent acts that are undertaken in order to get money for drugs. Violence occurs as an accidental effect of economic compulsive violence.[10]

Peter Hoaken and Sherry Stewart say that violent behavior may occur with stimulants because individuals who abuse stimulants may have a propensity to engage in violent behavior, or their aggression may result from withdrawal from the drug. They also say that violence may be a way to gain access to stimulants, or stimulants may exacerbate psychotic symptoms and lead to violent behavior.[11]

4

Amphetamine and Methamphetamine Abuse and Addiction

Jack, age 25, was addicted to methamphetamine, and he especially liked the sexual high that he felt when he took the drug and had sex with one or more partners. In fact, although he knew that meth was bad for him and he also knew that he was too thin and that most of his old friends avoided him now, in his mind, sex was directly linked to the use of meth and he was afraid that sex would become boring if he gave up the drug. And he liked having lots of sex and feeling high much of the time. Jack was not ready to give up meth.

Addiction to amphetamines causes significant changes to the brain and the body, and they aren't good changes. In addition, if the individual attempts on his or her own to withdraw from the drug, severe withdrawal symptoms, such as hallucinations and seizures, can occur. This is why it is best to withdraw from amphetamines under the treatment of an experienced addiction physician, who can help the individual transition to recovery.

Most people who abuse methamphetamine and other forms of amphetamines also abuse other drugs; for example, according to SAMHSA data, 37% of those admitted for methamphetamine treatment are also abusers of marijuana or hashish, while 31% abuse alcohol.[1]

PHYSICAL EFFECTS OF AMPHETAMINE/METHAMPHETAMINE ABUSE AND DEPENDENCE

The abuse of or dependence on amphetamine or methamphetamine can cause major physical changes to the body. Immediate results that are common include lack of appetite, insomnia, dilated (noticeably enlarged) pupils of the eyes, acne, uncontrollable muscle jerking, and dry and itchy skin. If an addict withdraws from amphetamine, this withdrawal leads to many opposite results, such as extreme hunger and appetite, depression, anxiety, and severe fatigue and exhaustion. The regular and chronic use of amphetamines can also lead to a worsening of present tics or the development of tics.

Heart Disease and Stroke

Deaths from heart disease and stroke have been reported in amphetamine abusers. For example, in a study in Texas of more than 3 million hospital discharges from January 1, 2000, to December 31, 2003, researcher Arthur N. Westover, M.D., and colleagues identified nearly 2,000 individuals ages 18 to 44 who were diagnosed with stroke. They found that amphetamine abuse was associated with a two times greater risk of hemorrhagic stroke than cocaine abuse. In addition, amphetamine abusers had a significantly greater risk of death after a hemorrhagic stroke than cocaine abusers.[2]

Figure 4.1 Amphetamines such as methamphetamine dramatically age and ravage the bodies of those who abuse it. *(© Multnomah County Sheriff's Office)*

In a case report of six young adults who died from chronic amphetamine abuse in Belgium, author Werner Jacobs, M.D, Ph.D., said that amphetamine cardiotoxicity was a rare but genuine problem that should be considered as a possibility by emergency rooms in symptomatic patients as well as in forensic (criminal) cases. For example, in one case, a 31-year-old man was found dead and lying on his back. White powder was found nearby and it was later identified as amphetamine. The autopsy showed that the man had extensive scar tissue in his heart and severe heart damage.

In another case reported by Jacobs, a 34-year-old dealer of amphetamines was found dead in his car in a parking lot. He had an enlarged heart with dilated ventricles of the heart, and a toxicology examination revealed amphetamines were present in the urine. The man had received treatment from a cardiologist, who stated that he had never considered that the patient may have been a drug abuser.[3]

In a much larger study in which the medical records of about 31 million U.S. patients ages 18 to 49 years nationwide were scanned for aortic dissection, a tear in the aorta of the heart that often requires surgery, researchers found that amphetamine dependence or abuse accounted for about 1% of the aortic dissections. They also estimated that amphetamine abusers had more than three times the risk of experiencing an aortic dissection as nonusers. Aortic tears are much more common in people ages 62 and older and they are unexpected in younger individuals.

Methamphetamine abuse is associated with the same effects as seen with amphetamine. In addition, methamphetamine users are at risk for stroke, which may occur as long as 12 hours from the last ingestion of the drug. Methamphetamine is a derivative or analogue to amphetamine and its effects can last up to 24 hours longer than those of amphetamine.[4]

Extreme Appetite Loss

The severe appetite loss seen with amphetamine abuse, particularly methamphetamine, is so extreme that some individuals develop malnutrition and they suffer severe weight loss. The lack of consuming a normal diet also contributes to the development of severe and obvious dental problems, often referred to as "meth mouth" because they are so common among methamphetamine abusers.

Meth Mouth

Meth mouth is caused by several key factors, including the drying up of normal oral fluids, and the failure to pay any attention to oral hygiene. Teeth grinding (bruxism) during sleep may also increase, worsening dental problems, and bruxism may occur for as long as 48 hours after the amphetamine was taken. This teeth grinding can chip the teeth.[5]

In a study of 301 adults who were dependent on methamphetamine and who were evaluated for diseases, researchers found that dental and oral diseases were the most commonly found problems, and were present in 41.3% of the subjects. The methamphetamine abusers also had more missing teeth than their non-abusing peers, 4.58 missing teeth versus 1.96 in the non-abusers. Nearly a quarter of the abusers (23.3%) had broken or loose teeth and 22.3% had problems with bruxism or tooth erosion. The intravenous use

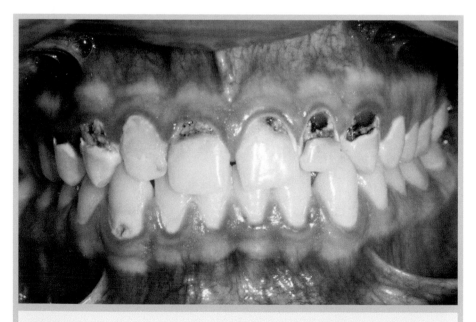

Figure 4.2   Meth mouth, or extreme tooth decay and damage, is caused by several factors, including the drying up of normal oral fluids, failure to pay attention to oral hygiene, and extensive teeth grinding (bruxism).   (© AP Images)

of methamphetamine was associated with a higher risk of dental problems than methamphetamine that was smoked.[6]

Sleep Disorders

Abuse of amphetamines can lead to a serious reduction in sleep, and may reduce the amount of time spent in rapid eye movement (REM) sleep, when dreaming occurs, by about 50%. It can also increase the time it takes a person to achieve REM sleep. If the person stops abusing amphetamine, then they are likely to be hypersomnic, sleeping up to several days without waking up.[7]

BEHAVIORAL AND PSYCHOLOGICAL EFFECTS OF AMPHETAMINE ABUSE

One potential effect of amphetamine abuse and dependence is hypersexuality, or increased sexual activity with decreased awareness of the risk for sexually transmitted disease or pregnancy. The person who abuses amphetamines may also develop psychotic behavior, which is known as amphetamine psychosis. This psychotic behavior may also occur with methamphetamine, an analogue or derivative of amphetamine. In addition, even stopping the drug altogether may not prevent later flashbacks, or the re-experiencing of symptoms of amphetamine or methamphetamine abuse as if the individual had just ingested the drug. According to Alasdair M. Barr and colleagues in their article for the *Journal of Psychiatry and Neuroscience,* individuals with recurring psychotic symptoms that were initially caused by methamphetamine abuse can improve by taking antipsychotic medications.[8]

Hypersexuality

Experts report that one consequence of the abuse and dependence on methamphetamine is that it escalates sexual behavior and also decreases the awareness of the consequences of sexual acts, such as the risks of contracting sexually transmitted diseases or creating unwanted pregnancies without taking precautions for safe sex. Methamphetamine also dries up the mucous membranes, including those body fluids that facilitate sex, and as a result,

Table 4.1 Comparisons of Behaviors Before and After Addition	
Before Addiction	**After Addiction**
Easily annoyed or angered	Goes into a blinding rage if irritated; small annoyances loom large
Adequate parent	Ignores children or may abuse them
Can and mostly does handle job requirements	Can't and doesn't want to work; work is no longer important
A few minor traffic tickets but no serious offenses	Felony convictions for drug selling
Mostly engages in safe sex	Forgets to use condoms; engages in practices like anal sex without condoms
Brushes teeth pretty much daily	Never brushes teeth; develops severe gum disease and loose teeth as well as clearly diseased mouth
Eats a normal diet	Forgets to eat for a few days or longer; develops vitamin deficiencies and malnutrition, looking like a starving person from a less developed country

some users irritate their genitalia because it has been rubbed raw because of the frequent and long-lasting sexual behavior in which they engage. Experts Arnold Washton and Joan Ellen Zweben say that this hypersexuality further increases the risk of unsafe behaviors. They note, "Regardless of the user's sexual orientation or gender, methamphetamine-induced hypersexuality is often associated with unsafe or high-risk sexual behaviors. Under the influence of methamphetamine, individuals are less likely to use condoms, more likely to have sexual encounters with strangers whose health status is unknown, and more likely to engage in vigorous unprotected vaginal or anal intercourse with multiple sex partners."[9]

Delusions

Delusions are false beliefs that seem real to the person who believes them. A belief that others are plotting against one is usually a delusion, especially if the individual believes a particular celebrity or political figure is after him or her. A belief that one is invulnerable and impervious to harm, and therefore that it is okay to jump off a tall building, is another example of a delusion. Delusional thinking is common among those who chronically abuse amphetamines.

Hallucinations

A hallucination is a false sensory experience that leads a person to see, hear, feel, smell, or taste things that are not there. For example, a hallucinating person on amphetamines or methamphetamine may imagine that insects are crawling all over the body and thus he or she must claw them off—in the process, causing harm to the skin. In the case of the methamphetamine abuser, this is such a common hallucination that it has its own name— "crank bugs."

ABUSE OF STIMULANTS DURING PREGNANCY

Some women who abuse amphetamines or methamphetamine during pregnancy do not realize that they are pregnant, while other women know they are pregnant but they continue to use the drug anyway. The use of stimulants during pregnancy can cause abnormalities to the fetus as well as miscarriage and premature labor. In general, pregnant women who abuse amphetamines are more likely to have complications such as anemia and a premature delivery.[10] Infants who are born to addicted mothers are themselves addicted and respond with repeated sneezing and shrill crying.[11] These infants also have a greater risk for being small for their gestational age and to have heart disease.[12]

A person who is hallucinating may also see people or others who are not really there, such as space aliens.

RISK FACTORS FOR ADDICTION

According to the NIDA there are four key influences leading a person to try drugs of any type and increasing the risk for addiction. First is the family, and if parents, siblings, or others in the home use drugs, a child has a greater risk for developing problems with drugs. The child's friends are crucial factors as well, and NIDA says that drug-abusing peers can sway even a child who has no other risk factors for drug abuse into trying an illegal substance.[13]

Another major risk factor is the early use of drugs, and research on every type of drug has shown that the earlier a person starts using a drug, the more likely it is that the individual will become a drug abuser or an addict. Last, smoking the drug or injecting it increases its high addictive potential. Thus, if a person smokes crystal meth or injects amphetamines, the rush occurs within seconds. It is this very euphoric feeling that the individual wants to experience, again and again, that leads to addiction.

WHERE PEOPLE OBTAIN AMPHETAMINES ILLEGALLY

Some people obtain prescribed amphetamines from friends and acquaintances, while others buy them through the Internet, sometimes using their presumably unknowing parents' credit cards to make the purchase. This is a strategy fraught with risk; for example, some researchers report that those who illegally sell amphetamines over the Internet sometimes substitute other drugs, such as antipsychotics and other substances that the consumers did not order.[14] As a result, purchasers don't really know what is in the drug that they receive in this manner. The drug may look okay, but is it? Maybe, maybe not.

Other individuals buy amphetamine and methamphetamine from street dealers, and clearly the purity as well as the content of the drug is in question when it is sold illicitly for a profit.

THE FDA IS STUDYING CARDIOVASCULAR RISKS OF ADHD STIMULANTS

Even among children, adolescents, and adults who are prescribed ADHD stimulants and who take the drug exactly as ordered, there may be associated cardiovascular risks. As of this writing, in late 2010, the FDA announced that the results of their review of about 2,000 medical charts of individuals taking stimulants were being evaluated for cardiovascular risks, and the results were expected to become available in 2011. If the FDA is concerned about potential cardiovascular risks in people who take stimulants lawfully and while under the control of a doctor, it seems logical to assume that the illegal use of stimulants would carry an even greater risk.[15]

From Friends or Acquaintances

Some people buy drugs from drug pushers, as with methamphetamine, but others find that it is relatively easy to receive amphetamines from individuals with legitimate prescriptions. In a study of college students who diverted their prescribed medications to others, either giving them away or selling them, the most commonly diverted types of drugs were ADHD stimulants, with nearly a 62% diversion rate.[16] This means that nearly two-thirds of students prescribed ADHD stimulants had diverted their medications to others.

Since people with ADHD who are prescribed stimulants can only obtain 30 days worth of an amphetamine or other stimulant at a time by federal law, it seems to beg the question of how they could have extra drugs to give away or sell. The answer may lie with poor medication adherence. One study showed that the average person with ADHD complied with what the doctor ordered only about 15 days out of 30.[17] If their noncompliance was in taking their medications only half the time, then this means they have 15 days of drugs left over every month, which would then enable them to have sufficient medications left over to divert their drugs to others.

Buying from the Internet

Some people obtain their illicit amphetamines over the Internet. In a study of stimulants marketed over the Internet for sale without a prescription, researchers Ty S. Schepis and colleagues found that this sale option presents a significant health risk, because buyers often don't really know what they're getting.[18] It's illegal to sell prescribed drugs to individuals without a prescription in the United States and anyone who would risk the penalties for doing so is unlikely to be concerned about the health and safety of the consumers who buy their products.

5
Addiction Treatment and Recovery

Davey's parents, family members, and former friends had staged an intervention, which Davey, age 17, thought was totally bogus, since he knew that he wasn't an addict. Sure, he liked to take amphetamines sometimes, like a few times a week or more, and when he couldn't get them by convincing or if necessary by threatening those ADHD kids in school, then he bought them off guys on the street, and sometimes he used his father's credit card to buy them on the Internet through some foreign Web site. But he was sure that he wasn't really addicted. That was just crazy talk.

Addiction experts report that an addiction to stimulants, especially a dependence on methamphetamine, can be very difficult to overcome. Those who are addicted to stimulants enjoy the euphoria that the drugs bring them, and to the addict, the highs of stimulant use are worth nearly any cost. As a result, the therapist must teach the addict to detach the joys of life from the use of methamphetamine and amphetamine, helping them learn that experiencing normal life with its ups and downs is a better way to live than depending on the feelings that stimulants induce as well as the many negative consequences that addiction can cause to their minds and bodies.

When individuals are treated for amphetamine abuse or dependence, there is no physical need to taper off the drug, as there is with some other drugs, such as benzodiazepines, and thus, the drug can be stopped immediately. However, the psychological impact is profound. For example, psychological symptoms peak within two to four days of the last use of amphetamine and many users have very depressed mood and talk about suicide.[1] Such severe reactions may require that the individual be admitted to a treatment facility and closely watched. Benzodiazepines (antianxiety medications) may help take the edge off withdrawal symptoms and thus may be ordered by physicians.

No medications have been approved by the FDA for the treatment of addiction to central nervous system stimulants, but some studies have indicated that the drug naltrexone can block craving for amphetamine.[2] Further studies will reveal if this medication can help stimulant abusers.

RESEARCH ON NALTREXONE AS A TREATMENT FOR AMPHETAMINE DEPENDENCE

There are no FDA-approved drugs for treatment of amphetamine dependence. However, some research has shown naltrexone, a medication approved by the FDA to treat alcohol dependence, is effective in treating dependence on amphetamines. In a study in Sweden, 55 patients addicted to amphetamines were treated with naltrexone or placebo. The researchers found subjects in the naltrexone group had a significantly greater number of amphetamine-free urine samples than the placebo group.

Naltrexone apparently blocks the "high" addicts receive from amphetamines as well as significantly decreasing craving for the drug. One subject in the naltrexone group who decided to "test" taking amphetamine during the study said she did not experience a high from the amphetamine and was surprised to feel that she was now free.

Further studies on naltrexone to treat individuals dependent on amphetamine should yield more information and ultimately may provide a treatment for individuals entrapped by their amphetamine addiction.

Source: Jayaram-Lindstrom, Nitya, et al. "Naltrexone for the Treatment of Amphetamine Dependence: A Randomized, Placebo-Controlled Trial." *American Journal of Psychiatry* 165, 11 (2008): 1442–1448.

ABUSE DATA BASED ON ADMISSIONS TO TREATMENT CENTERS

According to the Substance Abuse and Mental Health Services Administration (SAMHSA), most people who are admitted to treatment facilities for the abuse of amphetamine or methamphetamine began abusing the drug before age 21. For example, nearly 80% of the 142,184 people admitted to treatment centers in 2007 were children or young adults when they first started using. About 6% of these individuals started using stimulants at a very young age—when they were 12 years old or younger—and the largest percentage of users by age group included adolescents ages 15 to 16 years old, or nearly 18%.[3,4] In addition, about 7% of individuals admitted for dependence on methamphetamine or amphetamine were 19 years and younger.

However, the largest single group by age of individuals who were addicted to amphetamines, including methamphetamine and other amphetamines, were ages 25 to 29 years old, about 12% of all admissions. Interestingly, females were about twice as likely to be admitted for treatment for addiction to amphetamine or methamphetamine as the primary substance of abuse than were males—11.1% for females compared with 6.3% for males.

Considering Race and Ethnicity

In considering race alone, most individuals admitted for treatment of their addiction to amphetamine or methamphetamine in 2007 as their primary drug of abuse were Asian/Pacific Islanders (25.7%), Hispanic (11.6%), or white (8.7%). Only 1.1% of admissions were African American. Although 11.6% of individuals of Hispanic origin admitted for treatment for the abuse of any drug were admitted for the abuse of methamphetamine or amphetamine, the range among different ethnicities within the Hispanic category were very broad, proving that making generalizations about ethnic groups can be misleading. For example, the rate of treatment admissions was 21.6% for Mexicans compared to a low of less than 1% for Puerto Ricans. See Table 5.1 for more information.

Research provided by SAMHSA compared primary substances of abuse between male and female Mexican Americans who were substance abusers in 2007. They found that for females admitted to treatment, methamphetamine was the primary substance of abuse in 33.5% of admissions. Among males,

Table 5.1 Admissions by Gender and Race/Ethnicity to Treatment for Methamphetamine/Amphetamine as the Primary Substance of Abuse, 2007, by Percentage	
Gender	
Male	6.3
Female	11.1
Race/Ethnicity	
White	8.7
Black	1.1
Hispanic origin	11.6
Mexican	21.6
Puerto Rican	0.9
Cuban	4.2
Other Hispanic/not specified	8.4
Other Races/Ethnicities	
Alaska Native	6.6
American Indian	8.8
Asian/Pacific Islander	25.7
Other	16.3

Source: Substance Abuse and Mental Health Services Adminstration, Office of Applied Studies, "Differences in Substance Abuse Treatment Admissions between Mexican-American Males and Females," *The TEDS Report* (May 5, 2010). Available online at http://www.oas.samhsa.gov/2k10/226/226MexAd2k10Web.pdf. Accessed December 3, 2010.

methamphetamine represented only about half of the treatment admissions compared to females, or 17.8%.[5] The reason for this disparity is unknown.

Older Age Admissions for Amphetamines

SAMHSA compared the admission of individuals ages 50 and older by primary drug of treatment, comparing results for 1992 to those for 2008. Although still low, the admission rate for amphetamines among this older group rose from less than 1% (0.2%) in 1992 to 2.5% in 2008. In addition, in

Table 5.2 Percentage Increase in Rates from 1995 to 2005 for States with Highest Rates of Methamphetamine/ Amphetamine Admissions in 1995		
	Rate per 100,000 Persons Ages 12 and Older	Percentage Increase in Rate of Admissions
State	1995	2005	1995 to 2005
Oregon	281	314	12
Iowa	151	229	52
Nevada	112	174	55
California	111	218	96
Utah	110	208	89
Hawaii	107	244	128
Montana	89	185	108
Oklahoma	83	138	66
Washington	82	226	176
Arkansas	51	137	169

Source: Substance Abuse and Mental Health Services Administration, "Geographic Differences in Substance Abuse Treatment Admissions for Methamphetamine/ Amphetamine and Marijuana: 2005," The DASIS Report (January 17, 2008). Available online at http://www.drugabusestatistics.samhsa.gov/2k8/stateMethamphetamine TX/methamphetamines.htm. Accessed December 6, 2010.

considering any drug that was abused, the abuse of amphetamines rose from less than 1% (0.7%) in 1992 to 4.1% of those admitted for treatment in 2008.[6] The reasons for this disparity are unknown but may be linked to the overall greater popularity of methamphetamine in 2008 as compared to 1992.

State Treatment Rates for Amphetamine/ Methamphetamine Abuse

Some states have a high number of admissions for treatment for amphetamine or methamphetamine abuse, such as Oregon, Iowa, and Hawaii. For example, the rate of treatment per 100,000 persons ages 12 years and older in 1995 was 281 in Oregon in 1995 and rose to 314 per 100,000 individuals

WOMEN METH ADDICTS MAY FARE BETTER IN TREATMENT

In a study of 567 adult female methamphetamine addicts and 506 adult male methamphetamine addicts, all from California, the researchers analyzed improvements from intake to the three-month point and then the nine-month point after admission. Nearly all patients improved, but the researchers found that women improved more in the areas of family relationships and medical problems even though many women were unemployed, had children, lived with another person who used alcohol or drugs, and also had been physically or sexually abused. The women also reported more psychiatric symptoms than the men.

It was unclear why the women improved more than the men in some areas, although it may have been that the women were more highly motivated because of their children, or they may have been more responsive to treatment than the men. Services the women were provided such as public assistance may also have helped them with their recovery.[7]

by 2005. In addition, some states have seen a high percentage increase in the rates of admissions from 1995 to 2005, such as Washington State (176%) and Arkansas (169%). In general, abuse of these drugs is greater in Pacific and Mountain states, with the notable exceptions of Arkansas and Iowa. The reasons for these disparities are unknown.

COURT-MANDATED TREATMENT

Treatment for methamphetamine abuse may be court-ordered, as may treatment for amphetamine abuse. In fact, in looking at all types of treatment for all forms of substance abuse, SAMHSA reports that individuals who were referred to the criminal justice system for outpatient treatment are 58% more likely to complete their treatment than are individuals referred to treatment by another source. In addition, individuals admitted to short-term residential treatment by the criminal justice system are 37% more likely to complete their treatment than are those individuals who are referred by another source.[8] Clearly, avoiding incarceration is a motive to comply with court-ordered treatment.

TYPES OF THERAPY

Many treatment facilities use a combination of approaches to help drug abusers, as do individual therapists. The most common types of therapy used in treatment centers include substance abuse counseling, anger management, group therapy, 12-step facilitation, brief intervention therapy, contingency management/motivational incentives, cognitive-behavioral therapy, relapse prevention therapy, motivational interviewing, the Matrix Model, or community reinforcement that includes vouchers.[9] Nearly all treatment facilities for individuals with drug problems (96%) encourage the patient to talk about his or her individual experiences with the drug and also help the individual attain greater self-understanding of why drug use started and how it can best be ended.[10]

Anger Management

According to SAMHSA, anger management therapy is either always or often used by treatment facilities for individuals with all types of drug problems in 39% of the cases and it is sometimes used in 45% of all cases. Anger management is a form of therapy that generally uses a combination of other therapies, including cognitive-behavioral therapy and relaxation therapy, as well as teaching individuals better communication skills to help them recognize early signs of their anger and to deal with it appropriately early on, before they act in harmful emotional and physical ways to other people.[11] Since anger (and rage) is a common problem among chronic methamphetamine abusers and may also occur with amphetamine abusers as well, this approach seems to be a sound one.

Anger management therapy teaches individuals how to manage their anger with specific strategies practiced in group therapy. For example, if any member's anger starts to escalate out of control during a session, the leader can ask the member to take a time-out from the topic. In such a situation, the member and all other members of the group must immediately stop talking about the issue that induced anger in the individual. If despite this action the member is still very angry, he or she may be asked to leave the group for up to ten minutes in order to calm down.

The goal is to teach members to learn how to give themselves time-outs when they feel that they are losing control of their anger. Therapy can also help people rate their anger on a scale of 1 to 10 on the "Anger Meter," with 1 being a total state of calm and 10 being extreme anger that may lead to an assault or attack on others. Anger management methods help teach individuals to control their anger while they still can do so, before they blow up in a rage. When successful, anger management therapy helps clients master their anger and avoid escalations into aggressive acts of violence.[12]

People with anger management problems are also taught about those events or issues that trigger anger in many people, like being wrongly accused of something or having to clean up after another person. They are also taught specific physical cues to anger, such as feeling hot and flushed, as well as behavioral cues, such as raising the voice, slamming a door, or clenching the fists. Emotional cues to anger include feelings of guilt, jealousy, hurt, or fear. Cognitive cues are negative thoughts such as hostile self-talk or images of revenge or aggression. Individuals learn how to identify and deal with their own anger triggers.

Group Therapy

Many treatment facilities offer some version of group therapy, according to Arnold Washton and Joan Ellen Zweben in their book on cocaine and methamphetamine addiction. Say the authors:

> "Addiction is often characterized by the defenses of denial and self-deception. It also leads to isolation, shame, and impaired social functioning. Stimulant users, especially those with preaddiction histories of good functioning, frequently enter treatment with severely distorted ideas about themselves and the severity of their problem—issues that are dealt with very effectively in groups. Generally, new group members tend to overestimate their ability to deal with the problem on their own and underestimate their vulnerabilities. It can be especially difficult for these patients to accept the concept that they are unable to use drugs in a controlled manner and therefore must thus abstain completely, and that they need to rely on others to successfully overcome the problem."[13]

It is the group that helps individuals realize when they are deceiving themselves, because group members have been through many of the same types of experiences and self-deceptions themselves.

Figure 5.1 Group therapy is commonly offered at drug treatment facilities. (© *Photo Researchers*)

12-Step Facilitation

Twelve-step groups, most notably Alcoholics Anonymous, provide groups in which individuals announce their helplessness before their addiction and seek to work toward recovery in a 12-step process. Treatment facilities often encourage attendance at such groups and according to SAMHSA, 56% of treatment facilities either always or often facilitate membership in a 12-step group. There is no Amphetamine Anonymous group, but a Crystal Meth Anonymous 12-step group offers assistance to those who smoke methamphetamine. Some states offer pills to Anonymous groups for individuals addicted to prescription drugs, including amphetamines.

Some individuals object to 12-step groups because they believe they are religious or quasi-religious, but such organizations point out that they do not require belief in God or any gods. Instead, they are expected to surrender to a higher power, however they may define it to themselves.

Brief Intervention Therapy

Brief intervention therapy refers to therapy that provides from one to five sessions to individuals who abuse drugs but who are not yet addicted to them. The goal is to make the individual realize and accept that he or she has an escalating drug problem and to want to start to take the needed actions to resolve this problem, whether it is it by seeking substance abuse therapy or by other means.[14]

Contingency Management/Motivational Incentives

Therapy that involves contingency management and motivational incentives offers the drug abuser positive reinforcement (rewards) as they take steps toward recovering from their drug abuse. This form of therapy is always or often used by 27% of treatment facilities, according to SAMHSA.[15]

Cognitive-Behavioral Therapy

Cognitive-behavioral therapy (CBT) teaches individuals to recognize their own thought patterns and to then learn to challenge them in their minds. It also teaches them how to replace negative thoughts with more positive and behavior-enhancing thoughts. CBT is a common therapy in many treatment facilities and, according to SAMHSA, it is a therapy that is used always or often in 66% of cases and used sometimes in 25% of the cases.[16]

Relapse Prevention Therapy

Because many people who abuse or are addicted to drugs experience relapses after a period of abstinence, relapse prevention therapy is offered by many treatment facilities as a means to identify and correct problem behaviors.

SOME METHAMPHETAMINE ADDICTS ARE LESS LIKELY TO SUCCEED WITH TREATMENT

According to a manual offered by the California Department of Alcohol and Drug Programs in 2007, those clients who are less likely to succeed in either outpatient or residential treatment for methamphetamine abuse include those with less than a high school degree, those with a disability, those who are injection drug users, and those individuals with a very severe addiction.[18]

It employs cognitive-behavioral therapy to help individuals change their behavior. According to SAMHSA, relapse prevention is used always or often by 87% of treatment facilities.[17]

Motivational Interviewing

With motivational interviewing therapy, the therapist openly acknowledges that ambivalence (uncertainty and going back and forth with whether to make a change) is a common problem among people who need to make changes. The underpinnings of motivational interviewing is that this ambivalence itself is the key impediment to the drug abuser making the needed changes. The goal is not to focus on getting the person to make changes but rather to increase the individual's desire to make changes. Motivational interviewing is a counseling therapy that is always or often used in 55% of treatment facilities.[19]

According to Perry N. Halkitis in his book on methamphetamine addiction, motivational interviewing deals with issues that are present among drug users in the beginning of treatment, such as the aforementioned ambivalence as well as resistance and a lowered capability to objectively assess oneself. He notes that strategies within this form of therapy include empathy on the part of the therapist as well as the emphasis on client responsibility. This method is in contrast with methods used in past years that relied upon confrontations with the client. Motivational interviewing can be used in individual therapy as well as group therapy.[20]

The Matrix Model

The Matrix Model is an intensive program encompassing sixteen weeks of therapy and that combines CBT, motivational interviewing, and the involvement in a 12-step group, such as Crystal Meth Anonymous (which is modeled on Alcoholics Anonymous). The Matrix Model is always or often used by only 17% of treatment facilities for drug users.[21] It was developed in the 1980s at the Matrix Institute Clinic in southern California as a treatment to deal with an increasing number of methamphetamine users. This program includes individual counseling, relapse prevention groups, family education groups, early recovery groups, and social support groups. It also includes random drug testing weekly.[22]

Community Reinforcement that Includes Vouchers

An intensive outpatient therapy program, community reinforcement with vouchers is a system in which the drug user's family relations are emphasized

CHALLENGES IN TREATING METHAMPHETAMINE ADDICTS

According to author Richard Rawson, treating individuals addicted to methamphetamine is fraught with unique challenges. For example, many abusers who are new to treatment are resistant to treatment and are paranoid. In addition, they may misinterpret jokes or attempts at humor and see them as personal attacks. Patients may have thinking difficulties created by the drug and the therapist may think a patient is resistant when he or she actually does not understand what they are asked to do. Reminder cards and written goals can help with this problem. It is also true that methamphetamine abusers may suffer from wild mood swings and may also experience depression, lethargy, and apathy. Patients need to be reminded that such feelings are common in early treatment and that they will abate.[23]

and the person is given vocational training so that he or she can obtain a job. The incentive program provides a system whereby the individual can earn points that could gain them vouchers that they could use to purchase items in a store. This model is much less commonly used than the others, and is only used always or often by 5% of treatment facilities, according to SAMHSA.[24]

FREE TREATMENT

According to SAMHSA, free treatment is available for many substance abusers, and about 60% of all individuals admitted for treatment in 2008 had no health insurance. Most agencies providing free care are private nonprofit organizations. The free facilities were also more likely to have specially designed programs for clients than programs that were partially free or that had no free care. It should be noted that even among the 6,500 "no free" facilities, about half of these facilities offered a sliding payment scale for eligible clients.

Table 5.3 Clinical/Therapeutic Approaches Used Always or Often, by Availability of Free Care: 2008			
Clinical/Therapeutic Approach	Percent of "All Free" Facilities	Percent of "Partial Free" Facilities	Percent of "No Free" Facilities
Substance Abuse Counseling	97.8	97.4	96.1
12-Step Facilitation	49.1	59.9	55.7
Brief Intervention	35.7	38.0	33.9
Cognitive-Behavioral Therapy	46.6	67.3	65.6
Contingency Management/Motivational Incentives	28.1	29.7	25.3
Motivational Interviewing	51.2	57.9	48.4
Trauma-related Counseling	21.1	23.7	18.9
Anger Management	37.3	43.6	35.3
Matrix Model	10.8	17.5	13.0
Community Reinforcement Plus Vouchers	8.9	6.4	3.6
Rational Emotive Behavioral Therapy (REBT)	12.6	16.9	18.0
Relapse Prevention	88.6	90.0	87.2

Source: Substance Abuse and Mental Health Services Administration, "Free Substance Abuse Treatment," *The N-SSATS Report* (April 15, 2010), p. 4. Available online at http://www.oas.samhsa.gov/2k10/202/202FreeTx2k10Web.pdf. Accessed December 15, 2010.

Table 5.4 Programs or Groups for Specific Client Types, by Availability of Free Care			
Programs for Special Groups	Percent of "All Free" Facilities	Percent of "Partial Free" Facilities	Percent of "No-Free" Facilities
Driving Under the Influence/ Driving While Intoxicated (DUI/ DWI)	5.2	28.5	30.5
Adolescents	51.9	66.9	57.4
Clients with Co-occurring Mental and Substance Abuse Disorders	30.7	44.4	36.0
Criminal Justice Clients (other than DUI/DWI)	22.1	33.5	27.5
Persons with HIV or AIDs	10.3	12.4	7.8
Gays or Lesbians	4.6	6.7	5.1
Seniors or Older Adults	6.7	8.8	6.6
Adult Women	41.5	43.5	31.4
Pregnant or Postpartum Women	19.9	20.1	13.3
Adult Men	45.5	33.9	24.5
Source: Substance Abuse and Mental Health Services Administration, "Free Substance Abuse Treatment," *The N-SSATS Report* (April 15, 2010). Available online at http://www.oas.samhsa.gov/2k10/202/202FreeTx2k10Web.pdf. Accessed December 15, 2010.			

The type of therapies offered by the facilities varied by their availability of free care; for example, cognitive-behavioral therapy was more dominant among the partially free facilities (67.3%) and "no free" facilities (65.6%) than the "all free" facilities (46.6%). Services that the facilities offered particular types of clients varied as well; for example, 45.5% of substance abusing adult men received care in "all free" facilities, compared to lower percentages at other types of facilities.

Amphetamines and the Law

Jimmy, 17, was riding his skateboard home on the sidewalk when suddenly, a few hundred feet ahead of him, six police cars rushed in and came to a stop surrounding a small house set back from the street. Jimmy stopped in amazement and watched as the police raced from their squad cars, banging on the door of the house and shouting at the top of their lungs. No one answered, and the police used a battering ram to break down the door and then rushed in. Jimmy and others who were passing by wanted to wait and see what happened next, but a local police officer chased everyone away, telling them to go home, the show was over. On the news that night, Jimmy heard that the house the police had raced into was a clandestine methamphetamine lab. The landlord had apparently grown suspicious and contacted the cops.

Amphetamines that are abused may be diverted from legal sources, whether the drug is obtained from people with prescriptions for the drug because they have been diagnosed with ADHD or the drug is stolen from others. It may also be purchased from drug dealers or through an illicit site on the Internet. This is also the case for methylphenidate (Ritalin) that is abused. In contrast, most methamphetamine is created illegally in Mexico or in clandestine laboratories (sometimes located in the back of cars) in the United States, where law-breaking individuals use precursor drugs such as ephedrine or pseudoephedrine along with other chemicals to create methamphetamine for illicit sale to others. Methamphetamine abuse is closely linked to criminal arrests and incarceration, in part because federal and state officials are particularly concerned about methamphetamine abuse and also because of federal and state laws regarding the abuse of methamphetamine.

Sometimes the link between incarceration and drugs is tied to race and ethnicity; for example, researchers have found that American Indians/ Alaska Natives and Asians/Pacific Islander females are more likely than other groups to be referred to treatment for methamphetamine abuse by the criminal justice system, or 41% and 42%, compared to 33% of other races and ethnicities.[1]

Because of concern over drug abuse, many organizations require drug testing today, such as employers seeking to hire someone, law enforcement officials who test arrested individuals, and probation or parole officers testing individuals who are not incarcerated but who would violate their probation or parole if they tested positive for illegal drug use, risking jail or prison. Athletes in high school and college are also tested for drugs to ensure they have not gained an extra benefit to their performance because of drug use, as well as to deter them from drug abuse. In general, the types of drugs most commonly abused by student athletes as well as adult athletes are marijuana, steroids, and amphetamines.

Law enforcement authorities are also interested in arresting those who sell amphetamines and other drugs. In addition, forensics (criminal) experts are interested in the drug use of victims and perpetrators, to help prosecutors ascertain motives of crimes. For example, they may need to determine if a victim of homicide was murdered because the perpetrator was high on amphetamines or other drugs.

LAW ENFORCEMENT AND AMPHETAMINES

Most individuals who are chronic abusers of amphetamine or methamphetamine will eventually be arrested by a police officer and spend time in a jail or a prison cell. The arrest may occur because they are caught abusing an illegal drug or it may be tied to the commission of a crime, such as robbery, shoplifting, or prostitution that was committed in order to obtain money to buy drugs. It could also involve the crime of drug dealing. Once a person has acquired an arrest record for drugs, it is common for police to assume that in any other altercations with this person, drugs were also involved.

Another reason for an arrest may be the commission of a violent act, up to and including murder, as well as rape, assault, and other violent crimes. The individual may also be charged with child neglect or child abuse.

If the court finds that drugs were likely related to the crime, then drug treatment may be ordered. Alternatively, the person may be placed on probation and receive frequent drug tests. If he or she "fails" the drug test, meaning he or she tests positive for drugs, then it is a violation of probation and the person may be given a longer probation period or sent to jail or prison.

DRUG TESTING

Many organizations require individuals to undergo drug testing if they wish to be considered for a job and sometimes if they wish to stay on the job. In addition, individuals on probation for crimes often must undergo random drug tests and a failure—a positive drug test—is a violation of their probation and must be adjudicated in a court to determine if the individual should be given more probation or serve the jail or prison sentence that was foregone in lieu of probation. Parolees—individuals newly released from prison—often must also undergo random drug tests and a failure is grounds for return to prison.

The Department of Health and Human Services recommends testing for five substances, including amphetamine, marijuana, cocaine, opiates, and phencyclidine (PCP, angel dust). Amphetamines can be tested for up to 48 hours after the drug was ingested. According to pharmacologist Karen E. Moeller and colleagues, many drugs can give a false reading for amphetamines, such as the antidepressants bupropion (Wellbutrin), desipramine (Norpramin), or fluoxetine (Prozac), as well as pseudoephedrine (an ingredient in many cough and cold remedies), the blood pressure medication labetalol (Normodyne), the Parkinson's disease treatment drug selegiline (Eldepryl), the antinausea drug promethazine (Phenergan), and the anti-reflux drug ranitidine (Zantac). In addition, the antimigraine drug Midrin may generate a **false positive** test result for amphetamine.[2]

As a result, individuals who take these prescribed or over-the-counter drugs and who also know that they will be receiving a urine drug screening test should bring the prescription bottle or OTC medication to the testing site to show the tester, so that this information can be annotated in the record.

SIGNS OF A CLANDESTINE METH LAB

People who run illegal laboratories creating methamphetamine don't want others to know what they're doing, but there are some signs that may alert police and others to the operation of a meth lab in a house or other dwelling. Note: Anyone who suspects that a place might be a meth lab should not jokingly ask the people leaving the building if it could possibly be a meth lab. That could be a very dangerous question to ask a potentially paranoid methamphetamine producer, and could lead to physical harm or even death. It would be better to contact a person in authority with suspicions, such as a police officer.

Methamphetamine laboratories are very dangerous for the people using them as well as children in the area and others in the surrounding environment. Volatile ingredients are used to create methamphetamine, such as lithium from batteries, kitty litter, drain cleaner, and trichloroethane (gun cleaner), to name just a few of the noxious elements, in addition to the precursor drugs of ephedrine, pseudoephedrine, or phenylpropanolamine. Some individuals who make methamphetamine can become poisoned by the drugs they use in the manufacturing process and some may develop lead poisoning.

Indicators of a meth lab include the following:

- A pungent smell emanating from the area that resembles ammonia, cat urine, ether, or fingernail polish. The smell comes from the chemicals used to make the drug.
- An unusual amount of security for the neighborhood, such as barred windows and security cameras, when nobody else in the area uses them.

Drugs can be tested for in the urine, blood, hair, saliva, or sweat, although most organizations rely upon urine drug testing because it is usually cheaper and easier than the other choices. Saliva, as with urine, is a noninvasive means of drug testing. The fingernails or toenails can also be tested for drugs, but this method is rarely used.

- An unusual amount of trash for the area compared to the trash generated by others in the neighborhood.
- Dead vegetation in the area, caused by the fumes from methamphetamine.
- Few people coming to the area in the daytime but many people there late at night, often for brief intervals.
- Windows covered by blankets, boards, and other means.

Figure 6.1 A man in a protective suit and gas mask removes toxic supplies from a meth lab in rural Oregon. Meth labs are very dangerous, as toxic and highly flammable substances are used to make the drug. (© *Alamy*)

TESTING STUDENT ATHLETES FOR DRUGS

Student athletes in high school or college who fail drug tests risk losing scholarships and opportunities to play the sports that they love. The legality of such tests was upheld by the U.S. Supreme Court in 1997.

It has been argued that drugs can give students an extra and unfair edge in sports. It has also been argued that drug testing can serve as a deterrent to use of drugs by athletes, although some research indicates that this effect may be minimal. It is also argued by some that student athletes serve as an example to other students and if they abuse drugs, then other students will perceive drug abuse as behavior to be emulated.

Whether these arguments are valid or not, athletic drug testing is common and one of the key substances tested for is amphetamine (which includes methamphetamine). Other substances commonly tested for are marijuana, opiates, and benzodiazepines (antianxiety drugs, such as Ativan and Xanax).

ARRESTEES AND METHAMPHETAMINE

The Office of National Drug Control Policy of the Executive Office of the President reports on drug abuse among arrested individuals throughout the United States in the Arrestee Drug Abuse Monitoring Program, also called ADAM II. Arrestees are asked to provide information about their drug abuse, and most of those who report drug abuse are also tested for the drugs they have reported using recently to confirm they are telling the truth. The large majority are truthful on their drug use. For example in 2009, 86% of arrestees willingly provided a urine sample for drug testing. In the 2009 annual report, researchers concentrated on the abuse of marijuana (the most frequently abused drug), as well as the abuse of heroin, cocaine, and methamphetamine.

In considering methamphetamine alone, the researchers found that positive test results among abusers were the highest in Sacramento, California, where 31% of the arrested individuals tested positive for methamphetamine. The next highest rate was found in Portland, Oregon, where the rate of methamphetamine abuse was 13%. Other cities had much lower rates, of 1% or less, such as Atlanta, Washington, D.C., New York City, Indianapolis, and Charlotte, North Carolina. Thus, the severe methamphetamine problem appears concentrated in the Western United States.

The researchers also found that of those who used methamphetamine in Portland and Sacramento, the average use was 12 to 14 days per month. Most first-time arrestees nationwide were in their early twenties.[3]

INTERNET SALES OF SCHEDULED DRUGS

Some online Web sites offer scheduled drugs for sale, such as methylphenidate (Ritalin, Concerta), dextroamphetamine (Adderall, Dexedrine), and dexmethylphenidate HCl (Focalin). In a comprehensive report by the National Center on Addiction and Substance Abuse at Columbia University, in New York, the researchers noted that Internet users are largely young individuals, such as college students, teens, and even children. Illicit Web sites have few or no protections for children and in fact the researchers reported that a 13-year-old child, under the supervision of adults, ordered Ritalin online when giving her correct age, height, and weight.[4]

Of course, some online pharmacies are legitimate and most are certified by the National Association of Boards of Pharmacy under the Verified Internet Pharmacy Practice Sites (VIPPS) program.

In 2008, the researchers found 365 sites offering scheduled drugs for sale, a decrease from the 581 sites found in 2007. However, 27% of the sites sold stimulants, more than double the rate of 11% found in 2007. Many of these sites stay in business for a year and then close. The researchers also noted that legitimate payers are opposed to illegal drug sales; for example, PayPal does not allow purchases from a drug site unless the merchant has received a prior approval from PayPal. Only four such sites were approved by PayPal in 2008.[5]

Earlier research from the Substance Abuse and Mental Health Services Administration (SAMHSA) in 2005 found that about 7% of stimulant misusers obtained their drugs from the Internet.[6] Ty Schepis, Douglas Marlowe, and Robert Forman found that some Web sites were clearly favorable to the use of amphetamines, and these sites gave consumers examples of how the stimulant could help with doing better on an examination. Interestingly, the researchers found that, although amphetamines are available illegally over the Internet, drug sellers on the Internet generally steer away from selling crystal methamphetamine.

Said the researchers, "This study offers substantial evidence that multiple web sites offer to sell controlled stimulants without requiring a valid prescription. As predicted in the first hypothesis, eight of nine searched stimulants appeared to be offered online, with methamphetamine as the exception."[7] However, the researchers noted that instructions for making methamphetamine were widely available on the Internet. So these sites can tell users how to break the law, but it is the users who have to actually break the law themselves.

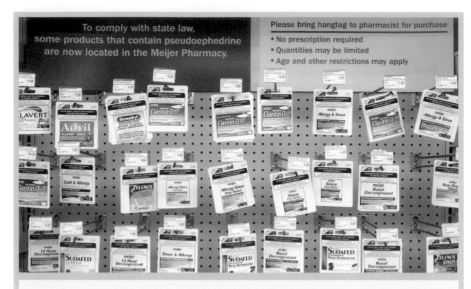

Figure 6.2   Laws sharply limit the quantity of over-the-counter drugs containing ephedrine that a customer may purchase at one time.   (© *AP Images*)

STATE AND FEDERAL CONTROLS ON PURCHASING SOME COLD MEDICINES

One way that the federal government has sought to gain control over the illegal manufacture of methamphetamine is to place strict controls over drugs that include ephedrine, pseudoephedrine, or phenylpropanolamine, in accordance with the Combat Methamphetamine Act of 2005. All of these drugs can be used as precursors to make methamphetamine. As a result of the law, individuals who wish to purchase such products from their local pharmacy must show identification and their data will be recorded to ensure they do not exceed the limit allowed on these products. According to the American Pharmacists Association, in October 2010, CVS Pharmacy was ordered to pay $75 million in penalties and also forfeit all profits earned from sales of pseudoephedrine because they failed to ensure compliance with laws that limit pseudoephedrine sales. The Drug Enforcement Administration said that most stores that sold pseudoephedrine illegally were in Los Angeles County and Orange County, California, and Clark County, Nevada.[8]

States must follow the federal laws but they may also enact laws that are even stricter than federal laws, if they wish. Some states, such as Oregon, have enacted laws requiring a prescription for any over-the-counter medications that contain ephedrine, pseudoephedrine, or phenylpropanolamine.

PRISON INMATES AND THE USE OF AMPHETAMINES

Some men and women in prison abuse illegal drugs when they can and methamphetamine and other stimulants, such as amphetamine and cocaine, are the drugs they seek.

In one study of 32 females who were incarcerated in prison and compared with 32 nonoffenders, the researchers studied the women's risk factors for imprisonment and they found that drug use, impulsivity, and sensation-seeking were significant factors that predicted a later incarceration. They also found that the female offenders were more likely than males to use multiple drugs and to be likely to have a substance use disorder related to stimulant abuse. In fact, the researchers found that a probable stimulant substance use disorder was the greatest predictor of incarceration among the women. The researchers hypothesized that stimulant abuse could cause long-lasting brain changes that then led to disinhibited behavior among the women.[9]

PENALTIES FOR DRUG POSSESSION AND SELLING

There are federal and state guidelines for the penalties imposed for the illegal possession of scheduled drugs. In general, possession of an illicit drug is punished less harshly than the production of and/or selling of illicit drugs. In addition, in the case of methamphetamine production, law enforcement officials and others analyze whether other people were harmed in the production of the drug and whether toxic chemicals likely contaminated the environment.

When considering penalties for drug crimes, prosecutors take into account such factors as whether this was a first offense or one of multiple offenses, the amount of the drug in question, and whether other crimes were related to the drug offense, particularly violent crimes. There is a complex system of points used by federal and state prosecutors to recommend a sentence for any given drug crime. In some cases, the individual may be sentenced in a special court known as a **drug court** and may be sentenced to mandatory treatment and completion of treatment in lieu of incarceration.

Because of the large number of prisoners incarcerated for drug crimes, which represent about two-thirds of all federal and state prisoners,[10] drug courts provide an option to crowded prisons. The first federal drug court was created in Miami, Florida, in 1989.[11] According to Jacqueline M. Mullany and Barbara Peat in their article on drug courts for *Criminal Justice Policy Review,* a drug court deals with cases involving addicted offenders and it offers a great deal of supervision as well as intensive treatment. Most participants in drug courts are male and they generally have poor work records and educational backgrounds and have failed past treatment. Most drug courts will not accept offenders with a violent past history or those who have violated parole.[12]

Drug courts have shown some positive results; for example, in one study, 10% of the drug court participants tested positive for drugs compared to 31% of those on probation and not in a drug court. Also, the retention rate in such programs is high; in one study the retention rate was 71%, or about twice as high as seen with other treatment retention rates.[13]

In an interesting study of pregnant women and drug crime, published in 2010, the researchers reported that marijuana and amphetamine were the primary substances for which pregnant women were sent to court-mandated treatment in 2004, a dramatic change from 1994, when most pregnant women court-ordered to treatment were addicted to cocaine (30.5%) or alcohol. This study included 3,486 women referred by the court for treatment in 1994 and 6,079 referred in 2004. There were 14,548 voluntary admissions for treatment in 1994 and 15,111 in 2004.

In considering amphetamine abuse alone and court-ordered treatment, the percentage of pregnant women more than doubled from 12.3% in 1994 to 27.6% in 2004. It is also interesting to note that the percentage of voluntary admissions for amphetamine abuse also more than doubled, from 7.1% in 1994 to 18.7% in 2004.[14] Clearly, amphetamine abuse was a greater problem for pregnant women in 2004 than in 1994.

The researchers had hypothesized that non-white, unemployed women using "hard" drugs would be the most likely to enter court-ordered treatment; however, their research found the opposite: White, employed women using either amphetamines or marijuana were the most likely to be referred to treatment.

The researchers also found that, over the entire study period, the rate of pregnant women referred to court-ordered treatment increased by 11.8% from 1994 to 2005, significantly greater than the 3.2% increase for men and the 7.8% increase for nonpregnant women.

SUMMARY

The lawful use of amphetamines as well as of central nervous system stimulants such as methylphenidate have greatly helped many children, adolescents, and adults diagnosed with attention-deficit/hyperactivity disorder (ADHD) or narcolepsy, a rare sleep disorder. At the same time, however, these drugs are sometimes abused by others. In addition, an illicit form of methamphetamine is a major drug of abuse in the United States today and it is highly addictive and difficult to treat, once an individual is addicted. A legal form of methamphetamine is available to treat ADHD but is rarely prescribed because of the stigma associated with the word *methamphetamine.*

The fact that some individuals benefit from taking a stimulant such as amphetamine or methylphenidate can lead to some erroneous conclusions by others. For example, some people may assume that amphetamines cannot be dangerous because they can be legally taken by others. However, central nervous system stimulants that are abused are nearly always taken at much higher dosages than are prescribed to people with ADHD. In addition, people taking stimulants under the control of a doctor can quickly report any problems and have their dosages adjusted downward or the drug discontinued or replaced.

Another erroneous conclusion is that stimulants are always bad, since some people abuse them. This was a belief held by some during the Prohibition period in the United States, when alcohol manufacture was illegal. The reality is that most people who consume alcohol do not become alcoholics, although some people do fall prey to this disease. Similarly, whether stimulants are used lawfully or sometimes even not lawfully, they do not always cause abuse or dependence, as with college students who abuse a friend's Ritalin to do better on a final examination. However, the risk for a fatal or serious heart attack is present with such diversion, and this health issue is of paramount concern.

The effects of stimulants can be profound, ranging from a racing heart to elevated body temperature to psychotic hallucinations and paranoia. In the worst case, death is the consequence of this form of drug abuse. Treatment is very important for those who abuse drugs, and can halt potential lifelong problems of severe health issues, anxiety, and violence.

Law enforcement is another major issue when it comes to the use of stimulants. Punishments for drug violations can be harsh, and the more violations, the harsher the sentence. Drug courts enable some adults with abuse and dependence problems to obtain needed treatment and end the revolving door of going in and out of jail and prison.

Appendix

Prescribed Amphetamines, Methamphetamine, and Amphetaminelike Stimulants

Generic Name	Brand Name	Ingredients	Amphetamine (A), Methamphetamine (M), or Other Prescribed Stimulant (O)	Year of FDA Approval for Treatment of ADHD
Methamphetamine	Desoxyn	Methamphetamine hydrochloride	M	1943
Methylphenidate	Ritalin	Methylphenidate hydrochloride	O	1955
Mixed amphetamine salts	Adderall	Amphetamine aspartate, amphetamine sulfate, dextramphetamine saccarate, dextroamphetamine sulfate	A	1960
Mixed amphetamine salts, extended release	Adderall XR			2001
Dextroamphetamine	Dexedrine	Dextroamphetamine sulfate	A	1975
Dextroamphetamine sustained-release capsules	Dexedrine spansules			1976

(continues)

(continued)				
Methylphenidate sustained-release capsules	Ritalin-SR	Methylphenidate hydrochloride	O	1982
Methylphenidate extended-release capsules	Concerta	Methylphenidate hydrochloride	O	2000
Methylphenidate	Focalin	Dexmethylphenidate hydrochloride	O	2001
Methylphenidate extended release	Focalin XR			2005
Methylphenidate extended release	Metadate ER	Methylphenidate hydrochloride	O	1999
Methylphenidate long-acting capsules	Ritalin LA	Methylphenidate hydrochloride	O	2002
Long-acting lisdexamfetamine dimesylate	Vyvanse	Lisdexamfetamine dimesylate	A	2007
Source: U.S. Food and Drug Administration, "Drugs@FDA: FDA Approved Drug Products," http://www.accessdata.fda.gov/scripts/cder/drugsatfda. Accessed February 2, 2011.				

Notes

Chapter 1

1. National Institute on Drug Abuse, *The Science of Addiction* (August 2010), http://www.drugabuse .gov/scienceofaddiction/ sciofaddiction.pdf (accessed September 7, 2010).

2. Carlton K. Erickson, *The Science of Addiction: From Neurobiology to Treatment* (New York: W. W. Norton, 2007).

3. Todd Zorick, et al., "Withdrawal Symptoms in Abstinent Methamphetamine-Dependent Subjects," *Addiction* 105 (2010): 1809–1818.

4. Steven M. Berman, et al., "Potential Adverse Effects of Amphetamine Treatment on Brain and Behavior: A Review," *Molecular Psychiatry* 14, no. 2 (2009): 123–142.

5. National Institute on Drug Abuse, "Stimulant ADHD Medications: Methylphenidate and Amphetamines," *NIDA InfoFacts* (June 2009), http://www.nida.nih.gov/ pdf/infofacts/ADHD09.pdf (accessed December 6, 2010).

6. Substance Abuse and Mental Health Services Administration, "Nonmedical Use of Adderall® among Full-Time College Students." *The NSDUH Report*, April 7, 2009, http:// www.oas.samhsa.gov/2k9/ adderall/adderall.pdf (accessed September 10, 2010).

7. Todd M. Durell et al., "Prevalence of Nonmedical Methamphetamine Use in the United States." *Substance Abuse Treatment, Prevention, and Policy* 3, no. 19 (July 2008), http://www.substanceabuse policy.com/content/3/1/19 (accessed September 10, 2010).

8. Arnold Washton and Joan Ellen Zweben, *Cocaine and Methamphetamine Addiction* (New York: W. W. Norton, 2009).

9. Substance Abuse and Mental Health Services Administration, *Results from the 2009 National Survey on Drug Use and Health. Volume 1: Summary of National Findings*

(September 16, 2010), http://www.oas.samhsa .gov/NSDUH/2k9NSDUH/ 2k9ResultsP.pdf (accessed September 17, 2010).

10. Ralph Weisheit, and William L. White, *Methamphetamine: Its History, Pharmacology, and Treatment* (Center City, Minn.: Hazelden, 2009).

11. Ibid.

12. Office of Diversion Control, Drug Enforcement Administration, "Drugs and Chemicals of Concern: Methamphetamine" (December 2010), http://www.deadiversion .usdoj.gov/drugs_concern/ meth.htm (accessed December 14, 2010).

13. Shoshanna Zevin, and Neal L. Benowitz, "Medical Aspects of Drug Abuse." In Steven B. Karch, ed. *Addiction and the Medical Complications of Drug Abuse* (Boca Raton, Fla.: CRC Press, 2007), 47–79.

14. Zevin and Benowitz, "Medical Aspects of Drug Abuse."

15. Weisheit and White, *Methamphetamine.*

16. National Institute on Drug Abuse, *The Science of Addiction.*

17. "Prescription Drug Abuse, Illegal Drug Use on the Rise." RedOrbit, http://www.redorbit.com/news/ health/1918823/prescription_ drug_abuse_illegal_drug_ use_on_the_rise/index.html (accessed September 17, 2010).

18. Alan D. DeSantis and Audrey Curtis Hane, "'Adderall Is Definitely Not a Drug': Justifications for the Illegal Use of ADHD Stimulants," *Substance Use and Misuse* 45 (2010): 31–46.

19. Ingebjørg Gustavsen, Jørg Mørland, and Jørgen G. Bramness, "Impairment Related to Blood Amphetamine and/ or Methamphetamine Concentrations in Suspected Drugged Drivers," *Accident Analysis and Prevention* 38, no. 3 (May 2006): 490–495.

20. Substance Abuse and Mental Health Services Administration, Office of Applied Studies, National Survey on Drug Use and Health, "Nonmedical Use of Adderal among Full-Time College Students," *The NSDUH Report* (April 7, 2009), http:// oas.samhsa.gov/2k9/adderall/ adderall.htm (accessed September 10, 2010).

21. Substance Abuse and Mental Health Services Administration, "Trends in Methamphetamine Admissions to Treatment: 1997–2007," *The TEDS Report* (October 1, 2009), http://www.oas.samhsa.gov /2k9/209/209MethTrends2k9_

web.pdf (accessed November 10, 2010).

22. Zevin and Benowitz, "Medical Aspects of Drug Abuse."

23. Nancy Nicosia, et al., *The Economic Cost of Methamphetamine Use in the United States, 2005*. Santa Monica, Calif.: RAND Drug Policy Research Center, 2009, http://www.rand.org/pubs/monographs/2009/RAND_MG829.pdf (accessed September 15, 2010).

24. Suzanne R. White, "Amphetamine Toxicity," *Seminars in Respiratory and Critical Care Medicine* 23, no. 1 (2002): 27–36.

25. National Institute on Drug Abuse, *Methamphetamine, NIDA Info Facts* (March 2010), http://www.drugabuse.gov/infofacts/methamphetamine.html (accessed September 10, 2010).

26. Ibid.

27. Zevin and Benowitz, "Medical Aspects of Drug Abuse."

28. Todd M. Durell, et al., "Prevalence of Nonmedical Methamphetamine Use in the United States," p. 4.

29. Zevin and Benowitz, "Medical Aspects of Drug Abuse."

30. Joel L. Young, *ADHD Grown Up: A Guide to Adolescent and Adult ADHD* (New York: W. W. Norton, 2007).

31. Christine Darredeau, et al., "Patterns and Predictors of Medication Compliance, Diversion, and Misuse in Adult Prescribed Methylphenidate Users," *Human Psychopharmacology: Clinical and Experimental* 22, no. 8 (December 2007): 529–536.

32. Ibid.

Chapter 2

1. Nicolas Rasmussen, *On Speed: The Many Lives of Amphetamine* (New York: New York University Press, 2008).

2. Charles O. Jackson, "The Amphetamine Inhaler: A Case Study of Medical Abuse," *Journal of the History of Medicine* 26 (1971): 187–196.

3. Rasmussen, *On Speed*.

4. Weisheit and White, *Methamphetamine*.

5. Nicolas Rasmussen, "America's First Amphetamine Epidemic 1929–1971," *American Journal of Public Health* 98, no. 6 (2008): 974–985.

6. Weisheit and White, *Methamphetamine*.

7. Nicolas Rasmussen, "Making the First Anti-Depressant: Amphetamine in Modern Medicine, 1929–1950," *Journal of the History of Medicine and Allied Sciences* 61, no. 3 (2006): 288–323.

8. Jackson, "The Amphetamine Inhaler."

9. Ibid.

10. Ibid.

11. Louise Sharkey and Michael Fitzgerald, "The History of Attention Deficit Hyperactivity Disorder," in *Handbook of Attention Deficit Hyperactivity Disorder,* Michael Fitzgerald, Mark Bellgrove, and Michael Gill, eds. (New York: John Wiley, 2007), 312.

12. Rick Mayes, Catherine Bagwell, and Jennifer Erkulater, *Medicating Children: ADHD and Pediatric Mental Health* (Cambridge, Mass.: Harvard University Press, 2009).

13. Sharkey and Fitzgerald, "The History of Attention Deficit Hyperactivity Disorder."

14. Mayes, Bagwell, and Erkulater, *Medicating Children.*

15. J. A. Dopheide, and S. R. Pliszka, "Attention-deficit-hyperactivity Disorder: An Update," *Pharmacotherapy* 29, no. 6 (2009): 656–679.

16. Lester Grinspoon and Peter Hedbloom, "A Historical Overview of Amphetamines." In Nancy Harris, ed., *The History of Drugs: Amphetamines* (Farmington Hills, Mich.: Greenhaven Press, 2005), 19–30.

17. Anonymous, "My Problem and How I Solved It: Addicted!" *Good Housekeeping* 164 (1967): 12–22.

18. Nancy Harris, ed., *The History of Drugs: Amphetamines* (Farmington Hills, Mich.: Greenhaven Press, 2005).

19. Rasmussen, *On Speed.*

20. Ibid.

21. E-mail communications with Michael Sanders, Special Agent/Public Information Officer for the Drug Enforcement Administration, September 22, 2010.

22. Grinspoon and Hedbloom, "A Historical Overview of Amphetamines."

23. Rasmussen, "America's First Amphetamine Epidemic."

24. Rasmussen, *On Speed.*

25. United Nations Office on Drugs and Crime. *Bulletin on Narcotics: A Century of International Drug Control* LIX, nos. 1 and 2 (2007): 90, http://www.unodc.org/unodc/en/data-and-analysis/bulletin_2007-01-01_1.html (accessed February 8, 2011).

26. Harris, *The History of Drugs: Amphetamines.*

27. Rasmussen, "America's First Amphetamine Epidemic."

28. Grinspoon and Hedbloom, "A Historical Overview of Amphetamines."

29. Rasmussen, "Making the First Anti-Depressant."

30. Ibid.

31. Ibid.

32. Henry M. Ray, "The Obese Patient: A Statistical Study and Analysis of Symptoms, Diagnosis and Metabolic Abnormalities. Sex Differences—Treatment," *American Journal of Digestive Diseases* 14, no. 5 (May 1947): 153–162.

33. Rasmussen, "America's First Amphetamine Epidemic."

34. Ibid.

35. Eric Colman," Anorectics on Trial: A Half Century of Federal Regulation of Prescription Appetite Suppressants," *Annals of Internal Medicine* 143, no. 5 (September 6, 2005): 380–385.

36. Charles F. Levinthal, *Drugs, Society, and Criminal Justice.* New York: Pearson Education, 2006.

37. Esther Gwinnell, and Christine Adamec, *The Encyclopedia of Drug Abuse* (New York: Facts On File, 2008).

38. Gwinnell and Adamec. *The Encyclopedia of Drug Abuse.*

39. Rasmussen, "America's First Amphetamine Epidemic."

40. Ibid.

Chapter 3

1. Perry N. Halkitis, *Methamphetamine Addiction: Biological Foundations, Psychological Factors, and Social Consequences* (Washington, D.C.: American Psychological Association, 2009).

2. National Institute on Drug Abuse, *Methamphetamine.*

3. Ibid.

4. Erickson, *The Science of Addiction: From Neurobiology to Treatment.*

5. William W. Stoops, et al., "The Reinforcing, Subject-Rated, Performance, and Cardiovascular effects of D-Amphetamine: Influence of Sensation-Seeking Status," *Addictive Behaviors* 32, no. 6 (June 2007): 1,177–1,188.

6. White, "Amphetamine Toxicity."

7. Neal Handly, "Toxicity, Amphetamine: Treatment & Medication," eMedicine (October 21, 2009). Available online at http://www.emedicine.medscape.com/article/812518-treatment (accessed December 12, 2010).

8. William L. White, "Substance Use and Violence: Understanding the Nuances of the Relationship," *Addiction Professional* 2, no. 1 (2004): 13–19.

9. Weisheit and White, *Methamphetamine.*

10. Sharon M. Boles and Karen Miotto, "Substance Abuse and Violence: A Review of the

Literature," *Aggression and Violent Behavior* 8 (2003): 155–174.

11. P. N. S. Hoaken and S. H. Stewart, "Drugs of Abuse and the Elicitation of Human Aggressive Behavior," *Addictive Behaviors* 28 (2003): 1,533–1,534.

Chapter 4

1. Substance Abuse and Mental Health Services Administration, "Trends in Methamphetamine Admissions to Treatment: 1997–2007," *The TEDS Report*, October 1, 2009, http://www.oas.samhsa.gov/2k9/209/209MethTrends2k9_web.pdf (accessed March 28, 2011).

2. Arthur N. Westover, Susan McBride, and Robert W. Haley, "Stroke in Young Adults Who Abuse Amphetamines or Cocaine: A Population-Based Study of Hospitalized Patients," *Archives of General Psychiatry* 64 (2007): 495–502.

3. Werner Jacobs, "Fatal Amphetamine-Associated Cardiotoxicity and Its Mediolegal Implications," *American Journal of Forensic Medicine and Pathology* 27, no. 2 (June 2006): 156–160.

4. Zevin and Benowitz, "Medical Aspects of Drug Abuse."

5. Zoe Hildrey, Sophie E. Thomas, and Alyson Smith, "The Physical Effects of Amphetamine Use." In Richard Pates and Diane Riley, eds., *Interventions for Amphetamine Misuse* (West Sussex, U.K.: Wiley-Blackwell, 2010), 9–25.

6. Vivek Shetty, et al., "The Relationship between Methamphetamine Use and Increased Dental Disease," *Journal of the American Dental Association* 141, no. 3 (2010): 307–318.

7. Hildrey, Thomas, and Smith, "The Physical Effects of Amphetamine Use."

8. Alasdair M. Barr, et al., "The Need for Speed: An Update on Methamphetamine Addiction," *Journal of Psychiatry and Neuroscience* 31, no. 5 (2006): 301–313.

9. Washton and Zweben, *Cocaine and Methamphetamine Addiction*.

10. V. Phupong and D. Darojn, "Amphetamine Abuse in Pregnancy: The Impact on Obstetric Outcome," *Archives of Gynecology and Obstetrics* 276, no. 2 (2007): 167–170.

11. National Institute on Drug Abuse, *The Science of Addiction*.

12. Adam J. Gordon, *Physical Illness and Drugs of Abuse:*

A Review of the Evidence (New York: Cambridge University Press, 2010).

13. National Institute on Drug Abuse. *Drugs, Brains, and Behavior: The Science of Addiction* (August 2010), 7. Available online at http://www.drugabuse.gov/scienceof addiction/sciofaddiction .pdf (accessed November 3, 2010).

14. Ty S. Schepis, Douglas B. Marlowe, and Robert F. Forman, "The Availability and Portrayal of Stimulants Over the Internet," *Journal of Adolescent Health* 42, no. 5 (May 2008): 458–465.

15. Food and Drug Administration, "Communication about an Ongoing Safety Review of Stimulant Medications Used in Children with Attention-Deficit/Hyperactivity Disorder (ADHD)," August 10, 2010, http://www.fda.gov/Drugs/ DrugSafety/PostmarketDrug SafetyInformationforPatients andProviders/DrugSafety InformationforHeathcare Professionals/ucm165858.htm (accessed September 15, 2010).

16. Laura Garnier, et al., "Sharing and Selling of Prescription Medications in a College Student Sample," *Journal of Clinical Psychiatry* 71, no. 3 (2010): 262–269.

17. Darredeau, "Patterns and Predictors."

18. Schepis, Marlowe, and Forman, "The Availability and Portrayal of Stimulants Over the Internet."

Chapter 5

1. Joanna Banbery, "Treatment of Withdrawal Syndromes," in *Addiction and the Medical Complications of Drug Abuse* (Boca Raton, Fla.: CRC Press, 2007), 23–32.

2. Nitya Jayaram-Lindström, et al., "Natrexone Attenuates the Subjective Effects of Amphetamine in Patients with Amphetamine Dependence," *Neuropsychopharmacology* 33 (2008): 1,856–1,863.

3. Substance Abuse and Mental Health Services Administration. "Trends in Methamphetamine Admissions to Treatment: 1997–2007."

4. Ibid.

5. Substance Abuse and Mental Health Services Administration, "Differences in Substance Abuse Treatment Admissions between Mexican-American Males and Females," *The TEDS Report* (May 5, 2010), http://www.oas.samhsa.gov/ 2k10/226/226MexAd2k10Web

.pdf (accessed December 3, 2010).

6. Substance Abuse and Mental Health Services Administration, "Changing Substance Abuse Patterns among Older Admissons: 1992 and 2008," *The TEDS Report* (June 17, 2010), http://www.oas.samhsa.gov/2k10/229/229OlderAdms2k10.htm (accessed December 3, 2010).

7. Yih-Ing Hser, Elizabeth Evans, and Yu-Chuang Huang, "Treatment Outcomes among Women and Men Methamphetamine Abusers in California," *Journal of Substance Abuse Treatment* 28 (2005): 77–85.

8. Substance Abuse and Mental Health Services Administration, "Predictors of Substance Abuse Treatment Completion or Transfer to Further Treatment, by Service Type," *The TEDS Report* (February 26, 2009), http://www.oas.samhsa.gov/2k9/TXpredictors/TXpredictors.pdf (accessed December 3, 2010).

9. Substance Abuse and Mental Health Services Administration, "Clinical or Therapeutic Approaches Used by Substance Abuse Treatment Facilities," *The N-SSATS Report* (October 14, 2010), http://www.drugabusestatistics.samhsa.gov/2k10/238/238ClinicalAp2k10Web.pdf (accessed December 3, 2010).

10. Substance Abuse and Mental Health Services Administration, "Clinical or Therapeutic Approaches Used by Substance Abuse Treatment Facilities."

11. Ibid.

12. Patrick M. Reilly, and Michael S. Shopshire, *Anger Management for Substance Abuse and Mental Health Clients: A Cognitive Behavioral Therapy Manual* (Rockville, Md.: Substance Abuse and Mental Health Services Administration, 2002).

13. Washton and Zweben, *Cocaine and Methamphetamine Addiction,* 85.

14. Substance Abuse and Mental Health Services Administration, "Clinical or Therapeutic Approaches Used by Substance Abuse Treatment Facilities."

15. Ibid.

16. Ibid.

17. Ibid.

18. California Department of Alcohol and Drug Programs, *Methamphetamine Treatment: A Practitioner's Reference, 2007.* Available online at http://www.adp.ca.gov/Meth/pdf/MethTreatmentGuide.pdf (accessed December 1, 2010).

19. Substance Abuse and Mental Health Services Administration, "Clinical or Therapeutic

Approaches Used by Substance Abuse Treatment Facilities."

20. Halkitis, *Methamphetamine Addiction.*

21. Substance Abuse and Mental Health Services Administration, "Clinical or Therapeutic Approaches Used by Substance Abuse Treatment Facilities."

22. Richard A. Rawson, "Treatments for Methamphetamine Dependence: Contingency Management and the Matrix Model." In Richard Pates and Diane Riley, eds. *Interventions for Amphetamine Misuse* (West Sussex, U.K.: Wiley-Blackwell, 2010), 83–99.

23. Ibid.

24. Substance Abuse and Mental Health Services Administration, "Clinical or Therapeutic Approaches Used by Substance Abuse Treatment Facilities."

Chapter 6

1. Substance Abuse and Mental Health Services Administration. "Trends in Methamphetamine Admissions to Treatment: 1997–2007."

2. Karen E. Moeller, Kelly C. Lee, and Julie C. Kissack, "Urine Drug Screening: Practical Guide for Clinicians," *Mayo Clinic Proceedings* 83, no. 1 (2008): 66–76.

3. Office of National Drug Control Policy, Executive Office of the President, *ADAM II: 2009 Annual Report* (Washington, D.C.: Office of National Drug Control Policy, June 2010).

4. National Center on Addiction and Substance Abuse at Columbia University, *"You've Got Drugs!" V. Prescription Drug Pushers on the Internet* (July 2008).

5. Ibid.

6. Substance Abuse and Mental Health Services Administration, *Results from the 2005 National Survey on Drug Use and Health: National Findings,* September 2006, http://www.oas.samhsa.gov/nsduh/2k5results.pdf (accessed March 28, 2011).

7. Schepis, Marlowe, and Forman, "The Availability and Portrayal of Stimulants Over the Internet."

8. American Pharmacists Association, "CVS to Pay $77.6 Million Penalty for Pseudoephedrine Sales" (October 15, 2010), http://www.pharmacist.com/AM/Template.cfm?Section=Home2&TEMPLATE=/CM/HTMLDisplay.cfm&CONTENTID=24469 (accessed December 16, 2010).

9. Caroline Brunelle, et al., "Personality and Substance Use Disorders in Female Offenders: A Matched Controlled Study," *Personality and Individual Differences* 46 (2009): 472–476.

10. J. Karberg and D. James, *Substance Dependence, Abuse, and Treatment of Jail Inmates, 2002* (Washington, D.C.: U.S. Department of Justice, Office of Justice Programs, Bureau of Justice Statistics, 2005).

11. Jacqueline Mullany and Barbara Peat, "Process Evaluation of a County Drug Court," *Criminal Justice Policy Review* 19, no. 4 (2008): 491–508.

12. Ibid.

13. S. Belenko, *Research on Drug Courts: A Critical Review—2001 Update* (New York: National Center on Addiction and Substance Abuse at Columbia University, 2001).

14. Mishka Terplan, et al., "'Compassionate Coercion': Factors Associated with Court-Mandated Drug and Alcohol Treatment in Pregnancy 1994–2005," *Journal of Addiction Medicine* 4, no. 3 (September 2010): 147–152.

Glossary

amphetamine toxicity An excessively high level of amphetamine in the body that leads to harmful reactions including, but not limited to, hyperthermia, heart attack, and stroke. The person with amphetamine toxicity urgently needs medical attention.

anhedonia A below-normal feeling of apathy and listlessness that is common in recent former amphetamine abusers and especially among past methamphetamine abusers. This is also one of the reasons why abusers return to the use of the drug. However, eventually normal feelings of pleasure do return after an end to the abuse of the drug.

crank A slang term for methamphetamine. It is said to derive from the late twentieth century, when motorcycle gangs hid methamphetamine in the crankcases of their bikes.

crank bugs Refers to a hallucination, experienced by some abusers of amphetamine and methamphetamine, in which they believe that bugs are crawling on or underneath their skin. The individual may tear at the skin in response.

crystal meth A smoked form of methamphetamine.

drug courts Special courts that manage the cases of individuals who are addicts or abusers of drugs. The court often mandates treatment.

false positive Occurs when a drug screen shows the presence of a drug even when the individual has not taken this drug. This result may occur when a person has ingested some prescribed or over-the-counter medications.

tolerance The need for greater amounts of an addictive substance in order to achieve the desired effects, such as euphoria.

yaba The Thai name for a tablet that combines methamphetamine with caffeine.

further Resources

Books and Articles

Darredeau, Christiane, et al. "Patterns and Predictors of Medication Compliance, Diversion, and Misuse in Adult Prescribed Methylphenidate Users." *Human Psychopharmacology Clin Exp* 22 (2007): 529–536.

DeSantis, Alan D., and Audrey Curtis Hane. "'Adderall Is Definitely Not a Drug': Justifications for the Illegal Use of ADHD Stimulants." *Substance Use & Misuse* 45 (2010): 31–46.

Durell, Todd M., et al. "Prevalence of Nonmedical Methamphetamine Use in the United States." *Substance Abuse Treatment, Prevention, and Policy,* http://www.substanceabuse policy.com/content/3/1/19 (accessed September 10, 2010).

Erickson, Carlton K. *The Science of Addiction: From Neurobiology to Treatment.* New York: W. W. Norton and Company, 2007.

Gordon, Adam J. *Physical Illness and Drugs of Abuse: A Review of the Evidence.* New York: Cambridge University Press, 2010.

Grinspoon, Lester, and Peter Hedbloom. "A Historical Overview of Amphetamines." In Nancy Harris, Editor. *The History of Drugs: Amphetamines.* Farmington Hills, Mich.: Greenhaven Press, 2005. Pages 19–30.

Gwinnell, Esther, and Christine Adamec. *The Encyclopedia of Drug Abuse.* New York: Facts On File, Inc., 2008.

Halkitis, Perry N. *Methamphetamine Addiction: Biological Foundations, Psychological Factors, and Social Consequences.* Washington, DC: American Psychological Association, 2009.

Harris, Nancy, ed. *The History of Drugs: Amphetamines.* Farmington Hills, Mich.: Greenhaven Press, 2005.

Jackson, Charles O. "The Amphetamine Inhaler: A Case Study of Medical Abuse." *Journal of the History of Medicine* 26 (1971): 187–196.

Mayes, Rick, Catherine Bagwell, and Jennifer Erkulater. *Medicating Children: ADHD and Pediatric Mental Health.* Cambridge, Mass: Harvard University Press, 2009.

National Institutes of Health. *The Science of Addiction.* August 2010. Available online at http://www.drugabuse.gov/scienceofaddiction/sciofaddiction.pdf.

Nicosia, Nancy, et al. *The Economic Cost of Methamphetamine Use in the United States,* 2005. Rand Drug Policy Research Center: 2009, http://www.rand.org/pubs/monographs/2009/RAND_MG829.pdf (accessed on September 15, 2010).

Pates, Richard, and Diane Riley, eds. *Interventions for Amphetamine Misuse.* West Sussex, United Kingdom: Wiley-Blackwell, 2010.

Rasmussen, Nicolas. *On Speed: The Many Lives of Amphetamine.* New York: New York University Press, 2008.

Rose, Mark. "Methamphetamine Abuse and Dependence." Continuing Medical Education Resource, Sacramento, California, http://www.netce.com/492/Course_5181.pdf (accessed December 1, 2010).

Sharkey, Louise, and Michael Fitzgerald. "The History of Attention Deficit Hyperactivity Disorder." In Michael Fitzgerald, Mark Bellgrove, and Michael Gill, Editors. *Handbook of Attention Deficit Hyperactivity Disorder.* New York: John Wiley & Sons, 2007.

Substance Abuse and Mental Health Services Administration. "Clinical or Therapeutic Approaches Used by Substance Abuse Treatment Facilities." *The N-SSATS Report.* October 14, 2010, http://www.drugabusestatistics.samhsa.gov/2k10/238/238ClinicalAp2k10Web.pdf (accessed December 3, 2010).

Substance Abuse and Mental Health Services Administration. "Trends in Methamphetamine Admissions to Treatment: 1997–2007." *The TEDS Report.* October 1, 2009, http://oas.samhsa.gov/2k9/209/209MethTrends2k9_web.pdf (accessed November 10, 2010).

Substance Abuse and Mental Health Services Administration. Results from the 2009 National Survey on Drug use and Health. Volume 1: Summary of National Findings, September 16, 2010, http://oas.samhsa.gov/NSDUH/2k9NSDUH/2k9ResultsP.pdf (accessed September 17, 2010).

United Nations Office on Drugs and Crime. *Bulletin on Narcotics: A Century of International Drug Control* LIX, nos. 1 and 2 (2007): 90.

Washton, Arnold, and Joan Ellen Zweben. *Cocaine & Methamphetamine Addiction.* New York: W. W. Norton, 2009.

Weisheit, Ralph, and William L. White. *Methamphetamine: Its History, Pharmacology, and Treatment.* Center City, Minn.: Hazelden, 2009.

Zevin, Shoshanna, and Neal L., Benowitz, "Medical Aspects of Drug Abuse." In Karch, Steven B., ed. *Addiction and the Medical Complications of Drug Abuse.* Boca Raton, Fla.: CRC Press, 2008.

Web Sites

Community Anti-Drug Coalitions of America
http://www.cadca.org

Crystal Meth Anonymous
http://www.crystalmeth.org

National Alliance for Drug Endangered Children
http://www.nationaldec.org

National Institute for Drug Abuse
http://www.nida.nih.gov

Pills Anonymous
http://www.pillsanonymous.org

Index

About the Author

Christine Adamec has authored and coauthored many books for Facts On File, including *The Encyclopedia of Alcoholism and Alcohol Abuse* (2010), *The Encyclopedia of Drug Abuse* (2008), *The Encyclopedia of Elder Care* (2009), *The Encyclopedia of Phobias, Fears, and Anxieties* (2008), *The Encyclopedia of Child Abuse,* third edition (2007), and numerous other titles on pivotal medical and psychological issues. In addition, Adamec authored *Pathological Gambling* (2010) for Chelsea House's Psychological Disorders series.

About the Consulting Editor

Consulting editor **David J. Triggle, Ph.D.,** is a SUNY Distinguished Professor and the University Professor at the State University of New York at Buffalo. These are the two highest academic ranks of the university. Professor Triggle received his education in the United Kingdom with a Ph.D. degree in chemistry from the University of Hull. Following postdoctoral fellowships at the University of Ottawa (Canada) and the University of London (United Kingdom) he assumed a position in the School of Pharmacy at the University at Buffalo. He served as chairman of the Department of Biochemical Pharmacology from 1971 to 1985 and as Dean of the School of Pharmacy from 1985 to 1995. From 1996 to 2001 he served as Dean of the Graduate School and from 1999 to 2001 was also the University Provost. He is currently the University Professor, in which capacity he teaches bioethics and science policy, and is President of the Center for Inquiry Institute, a think tank located in Amherst, New York, and devoted to issues around the public understanding of science. In the latter respect he is a major contributor to the online M.Ed. program—"Science and The Public"—in the Graduate School of Education and The Center for Inquiry.